THE BOLEYNS

of

BLICKLING

From Plough to Crown
in 100 Years

CHARLES WEIGAND

Bittern Books

First Published 2025

Bittern Books
Norwich NR10 5FB
bitternbooks.co.uk

ISBN 978-1-913415-50-1

Printed in the UK on paper from suppliers certified by the
Forest Stewardship Council® (FSC®) and the Programme
for Endorsement of Forest Certification (PEFC).

Contents

SALLE

Chapter 1
The Boleyns of Salle

In 1433, Geoffrey Bullen owned a few acres of farmland near the village of Salle in Norfolk.

In 1533 his great-great-granddaughter, Anne Boleyn, was crowned Queen of England

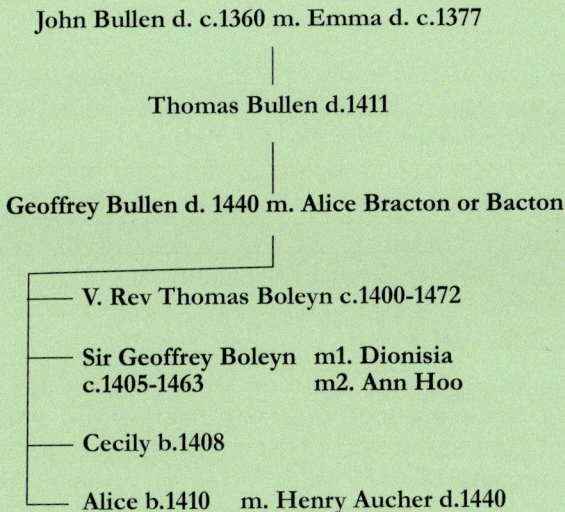

John Bullen d. c.1360 m. Emma d. c.1377

Thomas Bullen d.1411

Geoffrey Bullen d. 1440 m. Alice Bracton or Bacton

- V. Rev Thomas Boleyn c.1400-1472
- Sir Geoffrey Boleyn   m1. Dionisia
  c.1405-1463   m2. Ann Hoo
- Cecily b.1408
- Alice b.1410   m. Henry Aucher d.1440

Today we often hear talk of social mobility, but how, in the feudal and class oriented society of 15th and 16th century England, did the Boleyn family rise from their humble origins in Norfolk to the pinnacle of the nobility?

The earliest records of the Boleyn family in Norfolk indicate that they settled in the village of Salle possibly having come from France in the early 1200's. Their family name at that time, and often used throughout their lives, was Bullen. It was changed to Boleyn by Sir William in the late 1400s to make it more fashionable for the court. To avoid confusion, this book will mostly use the familiar spelling 'Boleyn'.

St. Peter and St. Paul Church, Salle, Norfolk

The first notation of the family in Salle was a Simon de Boleyne who had land in the village in 1252. There followed a John Bullen, possibly a son of Simon's, who was noted in 1283 in the register of Walsingham Abbey, then a prominent pilgrimage site. The next to appear was Nicholas, who was accused of theft in 1318.

Plague arrived in Norfolk in the 1350s and for the survivors new opportunities opened up. John probably died in the late 1360s, passing his leasehold land to his son Thomas. An Emma Boleyn who appears in the Court Rolls of 1377 was probably his widow.

In 1369 Thomas broke with tradition and purchased freehold land in Salle, then gradually acquired more, probably with income from the local worsted cloth industry[1]. Thomas died around 1411, leaving his land and house, known as Frothker Wood, to his son Geoffrey. Soon the Boleyn holdings (including leased land) extended beyond 40 acres which meant that they could use the title Yeoman.

It was with Geoffrey Boleyn, Yeoman, that the Boleyn family began their rise to status and prominence. They were now a prosperous family, selling wool and grains. He and his wife Alice, the daughter of Sir John Bracton [2], were major supporters and builders of Salle church, described as a small cathedral because of its size and quite a monument compared to the size of the village. The couple are shown in a brass

[1] Martin, Claire. *Heirs of Ambition*, pp 33-40
[2] There is no record of a Sir John Bracton and Claire Martin suggests this may have been a bit of creative genealogy in order to obtain a more impressive coat of arms. It is more likely Alice was the daughter of local family John Bacton and Martha Paston.

rendering inside the church: a very expensive indication of their standing within the village. Their new wealth also meant they could ensure their boys were well educated, a policy that was to pay dividends.

Geoffrey and Alice had at least four sons: Thomas (b.1400), Geoffrey (b.1405), William and John; and at least two daughters: Cecily (b.1408), born at Salle and buried at Blickling church and Alice (b. c.1410) who married Henry Aucher of Otterden (d. 1440) in Kent.

Thomas (c.1400-1472) became the prebendary of St. Stephen's, Westminster, precentor and sub-dean of Wells and 7th Master of Gonville Hall, Cambridge. He was the executor of his brother Geoffrey's will and had a gravestone erected for him with the words *Nowe Thus*, which was later taken as a motto by his grandson Sir Thomas Boleyn, Earl of Wiltshire, and his daughter Anne, second wife of Henry VIII. The Very Rev Thomas Boleyn was chosen by Henry VI in 1434 to attend the Council of Basel. His tomb is in Wells Cathedral.

William c.1376-1427 settled in Lincolnshire and was progenitor of the Lincolnshire branch of the family. He married in 1401 and had two children, but records are very scarce for this gentleman.

However, it was the second son, Geoffrey, who launched the Boleyn rise to nobility and influence through a combination of hard graft and a fortuitous marriage.

Wells Cathedral - Tomb of Thomas Boleyn, Precentor of Wells 1451-1472.
Image: Wendy Harris

Brass of Geoffrey and Alice Boleyn, dated 1440
Set in the floor of St. Peter and St. Paul's Church, Salle
The inscription (in Latin) translates as *"Here lies Geoffrey Boleyn who died the 25th day of the month of March A.D. 1440, and Alice, his wife, and children, on whose souls may God have mercy Amen"*

Chapter 2

Sir Geoffrey Boleyn and Lady Anne Hoo

**Sir Geoffrey Boleyn (or Bullen) of Salle and Blickling
Member of Parliament, Lord Mayor of London
and his wife
Lady Anne Elizabeth Hoo Boleyn**

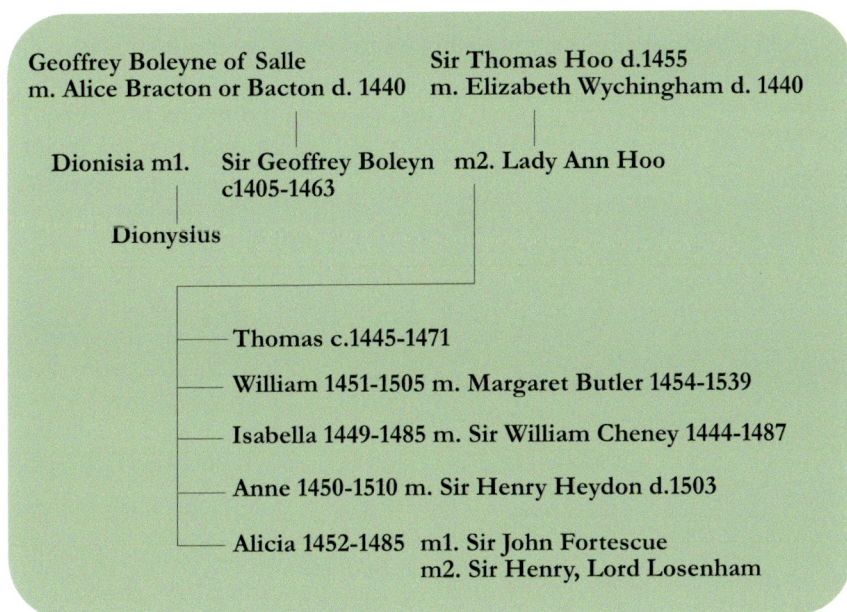

Geoffrey Boleyne of Salle   Sir Thomas Hoo d.1455
m. Alice Bracton or Bacton d. 1440   m. Elizabeth Wychingham d. 1440

Dionisia m1.   Sir Geoffrey Boleyn   m2. Lady Ann Hoo
                c1405-1463
      Dionysius

———— Thomas c.1445-1471

———— William 1451-1505 m. Margaret Butler 1454-1539

———— Isabella 1449-1485 m. Sir William Cheney 1444-1487

———— Anne 1450-1510 m. Sir Henry Heydon d.1503

———— Alicia 1452-1485 m1. Sir John Fortescue
                       m2. Sir Henry, Lord Losenham

The journey up the social ladder was seldom trouble free and invariably required the assistance of wealthy marriages, lucrative offices or good business acumen - or a combination of all three. The younger Geoffrey's wealth came principally from the latter, being a successful merchant, but was no doubt helped by a good marriage. He was an astute and clever London businessman, dealing with fine fabrics like velvet and silk, and became very wealthy in the process.

Geoffrey was born in 1405. His father ensured that Geoffrey and his brother Thomas were well educated, and at the age of around 16 Geoffrey was sent to London to take up an apprenticeship, most likely in the care of a man his father knew personally from their local hat manufacturing trade.[1] He was apprenticed to the Hatter Company and on completion of his apprenticeship in 1428 he became a Freeman of the City.

Around this time Geoffrey married Dionisia or Denise, his *'sometime wife'* according to his will[2], whose details are very sketchy. She died between 1443-45, probably in childbirth. There was one known child from this match, a son named Dionysius. He appears in the records, alongside his father and his uncle Thomas, as early benefactors of Queen's College, Cambridge. As his name disappears from the records it can be assumed he predeceased his father.

Geoffrey's marriage probably provided him with the funds he needed to set up on his own. In 1431 he made his first trip to the Low Countries (the Netherlands and Belgium of today) to purchase cloth and stock to bring to London, and so established himself as a merchant[3]. In February 1435 he transferred to the Mercer's Guild, London's premier livery company.

By 1445 Geoffrey had increased his fortune and reputation, and made his second marriage to Lady Anne Hoo, born c.1425 at Hoo Manor, Luton Hoo, Bedfordshire. She was the eldest daughter and joint heir of Sir Thomas Hoo and his wife, Elizabeth Wychingham. Geoffrey and Anne were married in Salle around 1445. He was twenty years older than her, but that wasn't unusual at the time. Geoffrey's prominence in the City of London, as well as the royal court, helped bring about this impressive marriage. He was seen as a rising star. Lady Anne was the first link into the nobility for the Boleyns.

At the time, prominent citizens were expected to serve in civic office, and in 1447, Geoffrey was appointed as Sheriff of London, an annual appointment. There followed a series of public appointments leading up to his term as Lord Mayor in 1457. Now he could mix with barons, bishops and chief judges. He sat on the royal council and was recognised by Henry VI with a knighthood.

The Hoo Family

Sir Thomas Hoo, Knight of the Garter (d. 1455), Baron Hoo and Hastings, was a leading Lancastrian courtier with great estates. Their main seat was Luton Hoo in Bedfordshire, but they also held land in Norfolk, notably Mulbarton.

Anne's mother was Elizabeth Wychingham (d. 1440), daughter and heiress of Sir Nicholas Wychingham of Witchingham in Norfolk.. Anne had three half sisters by her father's third marriage to Eleanor, daughter of Leo, Lord Welles: Anne, Eleanor (both married in their early teens) and Elizabeth.

Her father was made a Knight of the Garter in 1445 and ennobled by Henry VI as the 1st Lord of Hoo and Hastings in 1448. He fought with distinction in France, was the King's Keeper of the Seals and his Chancellor of France for thirteen years. His father, Sir Thomas de Hoo, won fame at the Battle of Agincourt.

---

[1] Martin C., *Heirs of Ambition*
[2] The will of Sir Geoffrey Boleyn, Probate 11/5/12, July 1463
[3] Martin C., p.63

This was a time of much political turmoil, as Henry VI was suffering from a mental illness which left him unable to rule the country for long periods. His wife Margaret of Anjou tried to take control, but Richard, Duke of York was made Protector. Eventually Henry was deposed and Richard's son was proclaimed King Edward IV in 1461. It wasn't until Henry Tudor won the Battle of Bosworth in 1485 that things settled down.

During this period Sir Geoffrey started to expand his property holdings, and after taking a house in London, he needed a country seat.

Where better than Blickling in Norfolk, just a few miles from Salle, and perfectly situated on the banks of the River Bure?

Sir Geoffrey purchased the Blickling estate from Sir John Fastolf in 1452 for £1,365 plus an annuity of £60 a year, a very large sum in those days. Blickling then became the Boleyn family seat where they replaced the existing wooden manor house of the Dagworth family with *'a fair house of brick'*. [1] He also built the chapel of St. Thomas at the east end of the north aisle of Blickling church, adorning it with beautiful painted glass that included his own and his wife's arms.

According to Sir John Paston, Sir Geoffrey did not readily pay the full price for Blickling, only paying Sir John Fastolf half.[2] Fastolf had to petition the King's chancellor, Cardinal Kemp, in 1452, to get this oversight resolved. This was probably a result of Sir Geoffrey, and four others, lending the King £1246 to help finance a military expedition to France.

In 1457 Sir Geoffrey bought the manor of Stiffkey, Norfolk with his brother Thomas and sister Cecily, and later acquired the Hever estate in Kent, combining the manors of Hever Cobham (named after Hever's builder, John de Cobham), Hever Brokays, from William Fiennes, Lord Saye and Sele, and Hever Castle from the Cobham family.

On the death of his father-in-law, Sir Thomas Hoo, in 1455, the Norfolk estate of Mulbarton (originally intended to be left to his wife, Lady Anne) was acquired by Geoffrey, and he went on to add the manors of Holkham, Filby, Postwick, West Lexham and Carbroke, all in Norfolk.

Sir Geoffrey died on 17 June 1463 in Middlesex Passage, London and was buried in the chapel of St. John, in the church of St. Lawrence Jewry, London, in accordance with his will. His death left Lady Anne a wealthy woman. In his will, he left her a significant share of his goods and chattels, including one half of his silver plate. He also left her all her own clothes, jewels and ornaments, something which was not usual

[1] Williamson T. and Dallas P., The Landscape of the Blickling Estate, pp.15-16
[2] Norton E., The Boleyn Women, p.21 – but original source Davis, N., The Paston Letters.

in the 15th century. He further left the huge sum of £1,000 for the poor householders of London and 1,000 marks[1] for each daughter.

Anne continued to manage the family estates until her sons came of age, and negotiated with her brother to inherit the Hoo family estates in Bedfordshire and Hertfordshire. She also bought a house in Norwich, which still exists, next door to what is now known as Dragon Hall in King Street.

Lady Anne died on 6 June 1484 in Norfolk and was buried in Norwich Cathedral where she was known to be a great benefactor. The Boleyn chapel in Norwich Cathedral was sponsored by Lady Anne and Sir Geoffrey. Initially, there were 17 shields depicting the Boleyns of Salle and Blickling, representing the seven families: Boleyn, Bracton, Hoo, St. Leger, St. Omer, Witchingham and Butler. Much of the chantry and its decoration were destroyed in the Civil War. Her son William was buried nearby.

Geoffrey and Anne had at least nine children. The Salle church brass denoting five sons and four daughters was in situ in 1730 but is now gone. It is quite probable that several of the children died before their parents. Listed below are those who were included in Sir Geoffrey's will, all being under the age of 25 and unmarried at the time (1463):

- Thomas (the eldest and heir, c.1445-April 1471). He died without issue in 1471 before he came of age to inherit, leaving his brother William as the next heir. Thomas was buried next to his father in London. Their chapel and burials were destroyed in the Great Fire of London 1666.

- William (c.1451-October 1505). Inherited the Boleyn estates in 1471 after the death of his brother. William's marriage to Margaret Butler, daughter of the 7th Earl of Ormond, ensured the Boleyn rise to prominence.

- Isabella, eldest daughter (c.1449-April 1485), buried at Blickling. Married Sir William Cheney (1444-May 1487) and had two sons: Francis and William. She has a brass in Blickling church.

- Anne (1450-May 1510). Married Sir Henry Heydon (d. 1503), Knight of the Bath. She was a wealthy widow and upon her death left legacies to Norwich Cathedral (where she was buried) and several Norwich friaries. One of Anne's children, Elizabeth, married a Hobart and another, Bridget, married a Paston, both notable families in Norfolk.

- Alicia, youngest daughter (c.1452 - April 1485) buried at Blickling. Married Sir John Fortescue and later Sir Henry, Lord Losenham. There were at least two children, Adrian and Mary.

---

[1] A 'mark' was worth two-thirds of a pound and was a commonly used term at the time, although it was never a physical coin. 1000 marks would be worth something in the order of £500,000 in today's money. (Source: measuringworth.com)

There is often mention of a possible son named Simon (b. c.1455, d. August 1482), who became the Chaplain of Salle church, but it appears he was unrelated (according to his own will). There is also mention of another possible daughter named Cecily but it appears that she was actually Sir Geoffrey's sister who died at Blickling in 1458, unmarried.

Lady Anne Hoo Boleyn died shortly before the Battle of Bosworth Field, August 1485, which ended the Wars of the Roses and the Plantagenet reign.

The Boleyns were now of the Tudor age.

Engraving of Blickling Hall by Prideaux, dated 1725

Chapter 3

Sir William Boleyn and Lady Margaret Butler

Sir William Boleyn
Justice of the Peace; Knight of the Bath; High Sheriff of Kent, Norfolk and Suffolk; 3rd Baron of the Exchequer, and his wife
Lady Margaret Butler Boleyn.

Sir Geoffrey Boleyn 1405-1463
m2. Ann Hoo

Sir Thomas Butler, d.1515
7th Earl of Ormonde
m1. Anne Hankeford 1431-1485

Sir William Boleyn
1451-1505

m Margaret Butler
1454-1539

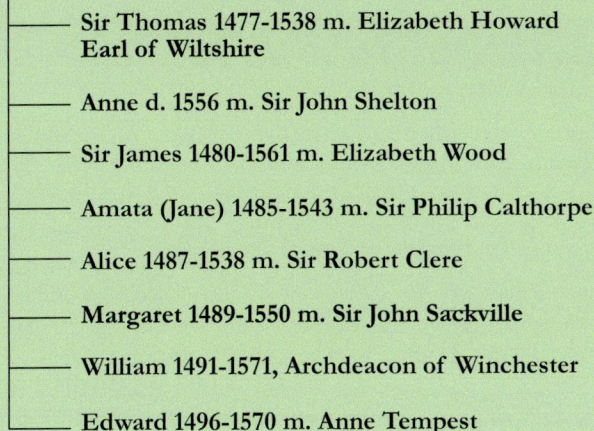

— **Sir Thomas 1477-1538 m. Elizabeth Howard Earl of Wiltshire**

— **Anne d. 1556 m. Sir John Shelton**

— **Sir James 1480-1561 m. Elizabeth Wood**

— **Amata (Jane) 1485-1543 m. Sir Philip Calthorpe**

— **Alice 1487-1538 m. Sir Robert Clere**

— **Margaret 1489-1550 m. Sir John Sackville**

— **William 1491-1571, Archdeacon of Winchester**

— **Edward 1496-1570 m. Anne Tempest**

William was the second son of Sir Geoffrey Boleyn and his wife Lady Anne Hoo, born at Salle on 30 June 1451.

Like his father, William was to become known as one of the 'new men' in society: those who had risen to prominence through wealth (mainly commercial), wedlock and ability. Both Henry VII and Henry VIII encouraged these new men as a way of limiting the power of the nobles. William was the grandfather of Queen Anne Boleyn and great-grandfather of Queen Elizabeth I.

William was married to Margaret Butler, daughter of Thomas Butler, the 7th Earl of Ormond. This very impressive marriage was arranged by William's mother and allowed the family to move in the same social circles as the prosperous Pastons, the Norfolk gentry, and the exalted Howards. It brought not only great wealth but a door to the upper nobility for the Boleyn family.

Margaret Butler was born in Kilkenny Castle, Ireland, around 1454 (her birth date is uncertain), younger daughter and co-heiress with her sister, Anne St. Leger, of Sir Thomas Butler, 7th Earl of Ormond and Baron Ormond of Rochford. Her mother, Anne Hankeford (1431-13 November 1485), was the daughter and co-heiress of Sir Richard Hankeford.

William and Margaret were married sometime before November 1469 when she is referred to as William's wife in a property agreement with Thomas Bourchier, Archbishop of Canterbury.

As a second son, William would have been expected to find his own path. Arrangements had been made for him to train as a lawyer at Lincoln's Inn, but that changed in 1472 when Thomas, William's older brother, died (probably in battle). William therefore inherited the Boleyn estate built up by his father, on coming of age at 25 in 1476.

In July 1483 William was created a Knight of the Bath at the coronation of Richard III. He is assumed, though not proved, to have been part of the Duke of Norfolk's forces supporting Richard III at the Battle of Bosworth in July 1485. He was able to return peacefully to Norfolk afterwards without suspicion.

Most of Sir William's life and career was in Norfolk. He was a member of the Commission of Array (a commission given by English sovereigns to officers or gentry in a given territory to muster and array the inhabitants and to see them in a condition for war) headed in the 1480s by the Dukes of Norfolk and Suffolk. In 1495, he was appointed to the *'Commission of Oyer and Terminer'* (the commissioners were commanded to make diligent inquiry into all felonies, treasons and misdemeanours committed in the counties specified) and closely connected to the commissions set up for the delivery of jails, bringing prisoners for trial at Norwich. He worked with other Norfolk knights to keep law and order.

Sir William is listed in the Norwich Heritage Centre records as owning the middle house, a four-bay hall called the Old Barge, on King Street, Norwich - presumably the house purchased by his mother, Lady Anne. The Pastons and Heydons lived nearby. It was sold before 1550, most likely by Sir James Boleyn who also sold the Blickling estate in the 1550's.

Sir William was installed by Henry VII as the High Sheriff of Kent in 1489 or 1490, and of Norfolk and Suffolk in the following year. This was the most prestigious, but expensive, office in the respective counties. The Sheriff was the representative of royal authority and responsible for the execution of law within the shire. He was also the Duke of Norfolk's deputy for the shires. William divided his time between Blickling and Hever for these offices.

Sir Geoffrey Boleyn had acquired Blickling in 1452, and the family mostly lived there until they moved to Hever in 1506. William finished converting Hever Castle into more grand living quarters, a process begun by his father. He is also credited with changing the family name from Bullen to Boleyn, a much more aristocratic name for the court.

At the Battle of Blackheath, Kent, in June 1498, Sir William fought for Henry VII against Cornish rebels alongside his son, Thomas, who was 21 at the time. He was charged by Henry to take care of the coastal beacons that were used to warn of an attack on England. Sir William and his family entertained Henry VII and his wife, Elizabeth of York, at Blickling in 1497.

He is listed continuously in Norfolk records from 1483 until his death in 1505. He only appears in the Kent lists for the years 1502-05, which coincides with his appointment in April 1502 as the 3rd Baron of the Exchequer, where he is named as William Bolling. Henry VII aimed to get a grip on the royal finances, which were in a terrible state upon his taking the throne. He only installed men with whom he had total trust. It demonstrates Sir William's prominence as he was knighted by a Yorkist king and advanced by a Tudor.

This was probably the most prestigious royal office Sir William held. The Barons were the chief auditors of the accounts of England. They were the judges of the English court known as the Exchequer of Pleas. Together they sat as a court of common law, settling, among other things, revenue disputes. There was one Chief Baron and upwards of four 'puisne', or junior, Barons.

William, Margaret and several of their children moved to Hever Castle, Kent in the 1480s to be closer to the royal court. William was described as a gentleman of Kent in 1489 though he maintained connections with Norfolk.

Margaret and William had a large family. Their first child, a daughter named Anne, died aged three in 1479, just before her fourth birthday. She was remembered by her parents with a fine memorial brass in Blickling Church. There was also a later daughter named Anne.

There were ten more children including six sons:

- Thomas (c.1477-12 March 1538/9), the future Earl of Wiltshire and father to Queen Anne Boleyn
- James (c.1480-5 December 1561/2), who would be the last Boleyn to live at Blickling
- John (1481-1484)
- Anthony, (c.1483-30 September 1493)
- William (c.1491-18 December 1571), who became the Archdeacon of Winchester
- Edward (c.1496-1570), who lived on his wife's estates in Yorkshire

Both John and Anthony died young and are buried at Blickling. Thomas, James and Edward were all knighted.

The daughters, all of whom were aunts to Queen Anne Boleyn, included:

- Anne (d. January 1555/6, buried at St. Mary's church, Shelton), married Sir John Shelton (1472- 1539), 21st Lord Shelton in 1497 at Blickling
- Jane (also known as Amata or Amy) (c.1485-1543, buried in Norwich) who married Sir Philip Calthorpe (1486-April 1549)
- Alice (1487-1 November 1538 buried Ormesby Saint Margaret, Norfolk), who married Sir Robert Clere, (c.1453-August 1529)
- Margaret (c.1489-1550, buried in Withyham, Sussex), who married in 1510 Sir John Sackville of Buckhurst (1483-1557)

Most, if not all, of the children appear to have been born at Blickling. Their arranged marriages to Norfolk gentry families reflected the social networks in which the family moved. Both Robert Clere and Philip Calthorpe were at the 1520 Field of the Cloth of Gold meeting in France between Henry VIII and Francois I of France.

Sir William died on 10 October 1505 at Hever Castle, Kent. His will was made on 8 October 1505 and proved on 27 November 1505. In it, he made charitable donations to Norwich Cathedral and Blickling church. He also willed that his son Thomas should have the manor of Blickling, in accordance with the will of Sir William's father, Sir Geoffrey Boleyn.

Sir William was seen as a fond father, having left bequests to all his children in his will. William had himself buried in Norwich Cathedral,

Game of Thrones

The late 15th century was the period of the Wars of the Roses, between Yorkist (Plantagenet) and Lancastrian (Tudor) factions. The weakness of Henry VI, who suffered from a mental illness, left a vacuum that was variously filled by his wife, Margaret of Anjou, and his cousin Richard of York and Richard's son, Edward, who eventually took the throne as Edward IV.

1431	Henry VI crowned.
1445	Henry VI marries Margaret of Anjou.
1453	Henry VI insane.
1454	Richard, Duke of York made Protector.
1455	Battle of St. Albans, won by York who becomes 'Constable of England' and Protector.
1459	York defeated at Ludford.
1460	March (later Edward IV), Warwick and Salisbury invade England from Calais. Henry VI taken prisoner at Northampton, York claims the crown. Richard of York killed at Battle of Wakefield.
1461	Edward IV proclaimed king. Henry VI and Margaret in Scotland.
1465	Henry VI captured and imprisoned in the Tower.
1468	Warwick disgraced, changes sides.
1470	Warwick invades from France, Edward flees and Henry VI restored.
1471	Battle of Barnet. Warwick killed. Margaret defeated and captured at Tewkesbury. Edward IV restored, Henry VI executed.
1483	Edward IV dies, succeeded by his son, Edward V aged 12. His uncle, Richard, Duke of Gloucester, takes the role of protector. Edward and his brother, Richard, are lodged in the Tower (the 'princes in the tower') but disappear, probably murdered. Gloucester is crowned as Richard III.
1484	Battle of Bosworth. Richard III killed. Henry Tudor, Earl of Richmond takes the crown as Henry VII.
1509	Death of Henry VII. Henry VIII crowned.

near his mother Anne. Included in his will of October 1505 was the stipulation that Lady Margaret would be paid 200 marks per year[1], at Blickling church, for her own maintenance.

In 1515 Lady Margaret's father, the Earl of Ormonde, died and she inherited 36 manors, which included Rochford and New Hall, both in Essex. These provided a further 400 marks per year in revenue.

Her eldest son, Sir Thomas, assumed the responsibility of running Margaret's and her sister Anne's inherited Butler lands at their request. A letter from Margaret to Thomas makes this plain and she further states that she would come down to London if he needed her to help with the estates though she would prefer to avoid the travel (both sisters were at an advanced age at this time). This letter, and others,

[1] Worth perhaps £100,000 in todays money.

show a close, affectionate bond and trust between mother and her eldest son.

Lady Margaret was probably the last Boleyn to live at Hever Castle. It has been stated that she was incapable of handling her own affairs for the last twenty years of her life. In 1519 she was declared a 'lunatic', but with periods of lucidity: in June 1520, she attended the Field of the Cloth of Gold meeting between Henry VIII and Francois I as part of Sir Thomas Boleyn's retinue, titled as Baroness Boleyn.

Lady Margaret died at Hever around 1540 (once again, the date is not definite) some time after Thomas who had died at Hever in March 1539. She was approximately 90 years old and was buried in St. Peter's churchyard, next to Hever Castle, the same church where Thomas was buried.

William was a courtier rather than a man of trade like his father. He was primarily concerned and involved with county issues though he was no stranger to the royal court or the royal family. However, it was to be his son Thomas who would take the family's prominence to the international stage.

Lady Margaret brought prestige, wealth and pedigree to the Boleyn family.

Through the marriages of Sir Geoffrey Boleyn to Lady Anne Hoo, and Sir William to Lady Margaret Butler, the Boleyns were on their way up in both county and royal society.

The Old Barge House in King Street, Norwich
Photographed by George Plunkett in 1946. Subsequently the ground floor has
been replaced with a concrete construction to support the historic first floor.
George Plunkett's wonderful collection of photographs of Norwich can be
found at http://www.georgeplunkett.co.uk/

The Earl of Ormonde by Hans Holbein the Younger
Often considered to be an image of Thomas Boleyn, but now believed to be a
drawing of James Butler, the 9th Earl of Ormonde. Royal Collection.

Chapter 4
Thomas Boleyn and Elizabeth Howard

Sir Thomas Boleyn
Knight of the Bath; Knight of the Garter; Lord Privy Seal;
Viscount Rochford; 1st Earl of Wiltshire and Earl of Ormond;
and his wife
Lady Elizabeth Howard Boleyn
Countess of Wiltshire and Ormond, Viscountess Rochford

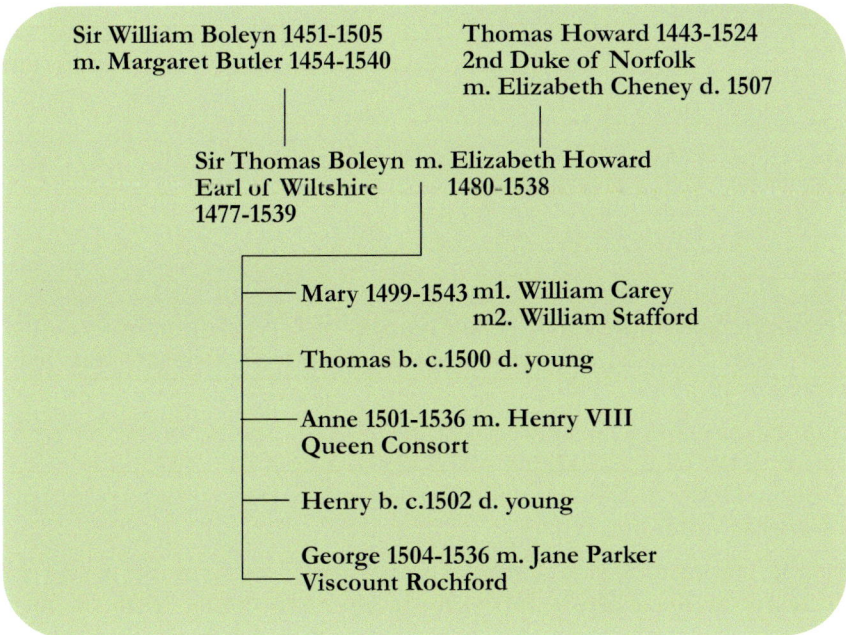

Sir William Boleyn 1451-1505
m. Margaret Butler 1454-1540

Thomas Howard 1443-1524
2nd Duke of Norfolk
m. Elizabeth Cheney d. 1507

Sir Thomas Boleyn m. Elizabeth Howard
Earl of Wiltshire   **1480-1538**
1477-1539

— **Mary 1499-1543 m1. William Carey**
                   m2. William Stafford

— **Thomas b. c.1500 d. young**

— **Anne 1501-1536 m. Henry VIII**
     Queen Consort

— **Henry b. c.1502 d. young**

— **George 1504-1536 m. Jane Parker**
     Viscount Rochford

Thomas Boleyn was an intelligent, hard working, clever, ambitious and capable man. His life was one of achievement, reward and ultimately great loss. He was born around 1477 at Blickling to Sir William Boleyn and Lady Margaret (Butler) Boleyn, their eldest son and heir, with five younger brothers and four sisters.

Thomas's early life was spent at Blickling and Hever, and after his marriage to Lady Elizabeth Howard his main residence was almost

23

The Howard Family

The Howard's were descendants of Sir William Howard, a chief justice of Common Pleas under Edward I. Their strategic marriages to East Anglian heiresses in the 15th century brought them considerable lands and wealth. They were strong supporters of the Yorkist kings Edward IV and Richard III.

Thomas Howard, Knight of the Garter and the Earl of Surrey, son of the 1st Duke of Norfolk and a powerful man at court. He was, at various times, the Lord Treasurer (1501), King's Lieutenant of the North, Lord High Stewart and Ambassador to the Holy Roman Emperor. He was a close confident and friend of Henry VII and Henry VIII.

Thomas and his father fought for Richard III at the battle of Bosworth Field in August 1485. The Duke was killed and Thomas was badly injured, captured, imprisoned in the Tower and lost all his lands and honours. Released in 1489, he was able to work his way back into favour with Henry VIII and was restored as the 2nd Duke of Norflok in 1514, and his son, also Thomas, made the Earl of Surrey.

The younger Thomas became the 3rd Duke of Norfolk on the death of his father in 1524, was a close advisor to Henry VIII and uncle to Queen Anne Boleyn.

certainly Blickling until the death of his father in 1505, when the family moved to Hever in Kent.

Lady Elizabeth Howard was the eldest daughter of Thomas Howard, the Earl of Surrey and 2nd Duke of Norfolk, and his wife Lady Elizabeth Tylney, Countess of Surrey, daughter of Sir Frederick Tylney.

Elizabeth Howard was born c.1480 at Arundel Castle, Sussex and was a descendant, via her paternal great-grandfather and maternal great-grandmother, of King John, Edward I and Edmund Crouchback, son of Henry III. She had three brothers (Thomas, Edward and Edmund) and two sisters (Elizabeth and Muriel).

Elizabeth remained with her mother throughout her childhood, becoming part of the royal court as a young girl. Like all female members of her class, she was raised for marriage (the advancement of the family). She received a very good education and was highly praised by the poet John Skelton for her beauty (fair hair, pale skin and blue eyes).

She was appointed a lady-in-waiting (c.1495) to Elizabeth of York, Henry VII's wife and Henry VIII's mother, and later to Catherine of Aragon, Henry VIII's first wife. She was considered an expert on court protocol in later life.

In the summer of 1497 the Boleyns were honoured by a visit to Blickling by King Henry VII and Queen Elizabeth of York on their way to the pilgrimage site of Walsingham in North Norfolk. Both Sir William and Thomas were present. Perhaps Elizabeth Howard was in the royal party.

In the same year, 1497, Thomas and William took part in the Battle of Blackheath, in support of Henry VII against the Cornish rebels. As far as we know this was the only military action Thomas ever saw.

Thomas and Elizabeth married around 1498 (although the date is not certain), probably at court where they had met. This marriage was a very good match for the Boleyns, made at a time when the Howard fortunes were not in the ascendancy (they had supported the Yorkists at Bosworth and lost their titles). It gave the Boleyn family entrance to the peerage, influence and prestige. For the Howards, it gave them needed wealth and a connection to an up-and-coming, ambitious courtier, Thomas Boleyn, in Henry VII's court.

Thomas and Elizabeth made Blickling their first family home, where (based on latest research) they had all five of their children – Thomas is recorded as saying they were having a child every year at Blickling:

• Thomas (b. c.1499, probably the first born son), died young.

• Henry (b. possibly as late as 1503), died young.

• Mary (b. c.1499)

• Anne (b. c.1501)

• George (b. c.1504)

The sons Thomas and Henry died young, probably from the dreaded sweating sickness which was endemic in Kent at the time of the family's move to Hever Castle in 1506. Both children are buried in Kent: Thomas in the Sidney Chapel of St. John the Baptist Church, Penshurst[1] (as 'Thomas Bwllayen') and Henry (as 'Henry Boleyn') in St. Peter's Church, Hever, beside his father's chest tomb. Their burials are very small, suggestive of very young children. The similar cross brasses on their burials, mentioned above, were dated stylistically by the Ashmolean Museum to 1520 when their parents may have had them made.

Lady Elizabeth has been described as proud and ambitious. She took charge of the education of her children and taught them, among other things, music, religion, arithmetic, embroidery, the family genealogy, good manners, household management, reading and writing. Both Anne and George became fluent in French. Their father was considered the most fluent in Henry's court - the family excelled at languages.

Meanwhile Thomas had become a prominent courtier for Henry VII. He was a trusted member of the King's court and was present at the marriage of Prince Arthur to Catherine of Aragon in 1501. He accompanied Lady Margaret Tudor, Henry VII's daughter, to

Henry VII

Lancastrian Henry Tudor had taken the throne as Henry VII in 1485 at the Battle of Bosworth, where Yorkist Richard III was killed, bringing years of civil war (the 'Wars of the Roses') to an end and finally establishing peace and stability in England.

By the time Thomas Boleyn came to court, Henry VII had two living sons, Prince Arthur (his heir) and Prince Henry, and two daughters, the Lady Margaret and Lady Mary.

---

[1] Why Thomas is buried at Penshurst and not Hever is an unanswered question. It is possible he was placed there by his parents to be educated in the running of a noble house, the 3rd Duke of Buckingham's in this case. Buckingham was beheaded for treason in 1521 and the Keepership of his palace was later given to Sir Thomas, where he apparently lived at times.

The Courts of Europe

In the 16th century there were three major powers in Europe, the French, the Holy Roman or Hapsburg empire, and the Pope.

The Holy Roman Empire was led by the Emperor Maximilian from 1486 to 1519 and included the modern territories of Germany, Austria, parts of Italy, Spain and the Netherlands. His daughter, Margaret, Duchess of Savoy, became Regent of the Netherlands and had her own court at Mechelen, now in Belgium.

Maximilian was succeeded in 1519 by his grandson Charles V, who also held the throne of Spain. Charles was the nephew of Henry VIII's first wife, Catherine of Aragon, and he was a great supporter of Catherine and her daughter Princess Mary and strongly opposed the divorce. Charles visited England in 1520 to meet with Henry.

In the French court the King, Louis XIII was succeeded in 1515 by his son-in-law Francois I, married to the young Queen Claude, Duchess of Brittany. Henry sought his backing for his divorce and the rulers met at the Field of the Cloth of Gold meeting in France in June 1520.

Pope Clement VII was from the Medici family and was head of the Catholic church and ruler of the Papal States (which comprised much of central Italy) between 1524 and 1534. His opposition to Henry's divorce led to England breaking from Catholicism. He was captured and imprisoned by Charles V's forces in 1527. Clement's successor was Pope Paul III from 1534 to 1549. He also refused Henry, and eventually excommunicated him.

Scotland for her marriage to King James IV in 1503 and became a Knight of the Body to Prince Henry (a bodyguard).

He was a pall bearer at the funeral of Prince Arthur and was Squire of the Body at the funeral of Henry VII, who died on 21 April 1509 at Richmond Palace of tuberculosis. These were all positions of honour, reflecting how highly the royal family thought of him.

In November 1505, Sir William Boleyn died leaving the estates of Hever, Blickling and a number of other manors in Kent and Norfolk to Thomas. Soon afterwards Thomas and family were given royal approval from Henry VII to take possession of Hever. Their main purpose for the move was to be closer to the court and the royal family. Thereafter, Thomas spent little time at Blickling: the court was his focal point so Hever became his primary seat. His brother James made Blickling his seat.

At the coronation of Henry VIII in 1509, Thomas was knighted and Elizabeth attended Queen Catherine. Thomas already knew Henry well and the new king was to use him extensively in his foreign affairs and the pursuit of his divorce from Queen Catherine.

Now 'Sir Thomas', he jousted with the King in February 1511 as part of the celebration of the birth of the King's son, Henry, Duke of Cornwall. Sadly, six weeks later he helped carry the child's body to burial in Westminster Abbey.

Henry VIII, like his father, saw in Sir Thomas a man with the abilities he needed to negotiate with foreign rulers, Henry's divorce and the major changes that were to come in the state religion. Thomas served as Henry's ambassador, first to the Emperor Maximilian in 1512/13, then to France in 1518-20 and to the Pope in 1530. He was well liked and welcomed in the courts of Francois I, Margaret of Austria, Charles V and the Pope. He was on very good terms with Margaret and upon his departure (c.1513), after a year at her court, she offered his daughter Anne a place in her finishing school. Anne would have been 12 or 13 at the time, the accepted age to begin this training.

As Ambassador to France, Sir Thomas was directly involved in the negotiations and preparations for the June 1520 meeting of Henry and Francois I of France, known as the The Field of the Cloth of Gold, and rode with Henry at the embracing of the two kings, a great honour. Thomas was about 43 years old then.

In addition to these important positions, Sir Thomas was also appointed Joint Constable of Norwich Castle in 1511/12, Sheriff of Kent in November 1517, Privy Councillor in 1518, and was invested as a Knight of the Garter in 1523.

The Field of the Cloth of Gold

In June 1520, a summit meeting was arranged between Henry VIII and King Francois I of France. It was held at Balingham, just outside Calais, which was the last English stronghold on the continent, left over from the Hundred Years War (1337-1453).

The summit was arranged by Cardinal Thomas Wolsey who hoped it would increase the bond of friendship between the two kings, a follow-on from the Anglo-French treaty of 1514 which sought to 'outlaw' war among Christian states. France wanted to engage England as an ally against Charles V, the Holy Roman Emperor, although unbeknownst to Francois, Henry was also negotiating with Charles.

A majority of Henry's court were in attendance, including most of the Boleyn family. A very elaborate and hugely expensive programme had been organised with each king trying to outshine the other in jousting, wrestling, music, clothing and huge feasts and games. Henry even brought 2 monkeys covered in gold leaf which Francois found very amusing. The 2,800 tents and costumes had so much fabric woven with silk and gold thread the summit became known as the Field of the Cloth of Gold. But in the end the political results were negligible.

Henry then raised him to the nobility as Viscount Rochford on 18 June 1525, the manor of Rochford being part of his mother's inheritance from the Butlers. Four years later, the King granted Thomas his maternal grandfather's title, Earl of Wiltshire and Ormond and in 1530 appointed him Lord Privy Seal. He even had Thomas stand in for him as godfather at the christening of Francois I's second son, the Duke of Orleans, who was named Henry.

These advancements and recognitions were due to Thomas's abilities and not directly related to Henry's infatuation with his daughter Anne.

But as could be expected in Henry's court, Thomas's rise to power also brought enemies to the Boleyns.

In December 1526, Henry bought a ship named the 'Anne Boleyn' from Sir Thomas. In 1523 he had a 100 ton ship called the 'Mary Boleyn' in his navy. It appears both ships were owned and named by Thomas Boleyn.

Sir Thomas also owned a Thames-side mansion on the Strand in London called Durham Place. At times, it was made available as a home for Archbishop Thomas Cranmer while he was working on the King's Great Matter (his divorce from Queen Catherine).

Chapter 5
Mary Boleyn

Lady Mary Boleyn Carey Stafford

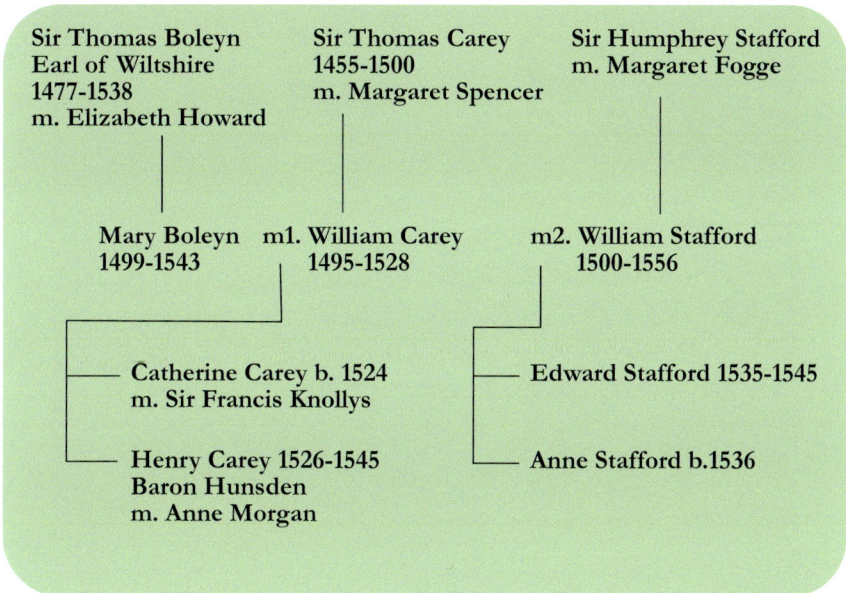

Sir Thomas Boleyn Earl of Wiltshire 1477-1538 m. Elizabeth Howard	Sir Thomas Carey 1455-1500 m. Margaret Spencer	Sir Humphrey Stafford m. Margaret Fogge

Mary Boleyn 1499-1543 m1. William Carey 1495-1528   m2. William Stafford 1500-1556

— Catherine Carey b. 1524 m. Sir Francis Knollys

— Henry Carey 1526-1545 Baron Hunsden m. Anne Morgan

— Edward Stafford 1535-1545

— Anne Stafford b.1536

Mary Boleyn was born c.1499 at Blickling Hall, daughter of Master Thomas and Lady Elizabeth Boleyn (Thomas wasn't knighted until 1509). The family lived at Blickling until 1506, when Thomas's father, William, died and they moved to Hever in Kent. Mary was almost certainly their first daughter, and may have been the first born child, although dates of birth of the children are not known for certain.

Sometime after the move to Kent, two of Mary's brothers, Henry and Thomas, died, leaving two surviving siblings: Anne (probably born around 1501) and George (born about 1504).

Mary was considered the prettier of the Boleyn sisters, with fair hair and blue eyes, although Anne was the more intellectual. Both sisters received a well-rounded and extensive education, which included French, religion, music, maths and history, and recreational activities

Mary Boleyn
Attributed to Remigius van Leemput (d. 1675) - Portrait of a Woman
(Public Domain)

such as archery, riding, and hunting. This was in addition to the more feminine pursuits of the time of dancing, household management, singing, and games such as cards and chess.

At the age of about 15 in the summer of 1514, Mary was selected through her father's efforts as a Maid of Honour for Princess Mary Tudor, Henry VIII's 18 year old sister, when she travelled to France for her marriage to the French king, Louis XII. Louis was 53, had had two previous marriages, with no male heir and was now suffering from leprosy - Mary Tudor was his last hope. Sir Thomas was also part of the train. Three months later Louis died without an heir and his cousin Francois took the French throne. Mary Tudor then secretly married Charles Brandon, Duke of Suffolk without Henry's permission.

Mary Boleyn stayed on at the French court and during the period 1514-1515, she was noted as being a mistress of the new king, something which stained her reputation with her family and the court. Her father recalled her from France about 1518/19. Mary's sister Anne had also joined the French court at this time to attend Queen Claude.

On 4 February 1520, Mary was married to William Carey, MP, Gentleman of the Privy Chamber and Esquire of the Body to Henry VIII, in the Chapel Royal, Greenwich. William was descended from Edward III and was a 3rd cousin of Henry's, who attended their marriage.

Both William and Mary were present at the Field of the Cloth of Gold in 1520. William distinguished himself in the jousting and Mary, now Lady Carey, was among the Household of Queen Catherine of Aragon.

William's abilities were recognised and in 1522 the King awarded him the position of bailiff of the manors of New Hall, Walkeford Hall and Powers (Hall End), Essex and keepership of the King's house, Beaulieu. In June 1524 he was given the keepership of the manor of Wanstead where he and Mary stayed many times. He was a rising star at court.

There were two children of this marriage: a daughter, Catherine (later to become Lady Knollys), born 19 May 1524 and a son, Henry (later 1st Baron Hunsdon, Knight of the Garter), born in March 1525.

It was during the period c.1522-1525 that Mary was a discreet though reluctant mistress of Henry VIII, which finished amicably prior to the birth of her son Henry. Both children were reputed to have been fathered by the King, though he never acknowledged them as his. He did, however, ensure they got a proper upbringing as can be noted in his expense records. Henry acknowledged his affair with Mary when he applied to the Pope in 1528 for a dispensation to marry the sister (Anne) of a woman (Mary) who had been his mistress.

As her father rather scathingly put it:

> *"She had not only compromised her honour a second time, but had not collected on her investment."*[1]

William Carey died of the sweating sickness on 22nd June 1528 at Pleshey Castle, Essex, but his burial place is unknown: it may have been a mass grave, often used during these outbreaks. Mary was now a widow and where she lived is unknown, but she attended the coronation of her sister Anne in 1533.

On 8th Dec 1529, Thomas Boleyn was created Earl of Wiltshire and Ormond which entitled Mary to call herself Lady Mary Rochford. Her brother George would assume the title of Lord Rochford the next year.

---

[1] Weir A., Mary Boleyn pg 240

Rochford Hall

Rochford Hall in Essex dates back as early as 1216. It was inherited by Sir Thomas Boleyn's mother, Margaret, upon the death of her father, Thomas Butler, Baron Rochford, 7th Earl of Ormonde. At that time, he was the premier baron of England and the richest.

Sir Thomas was to add extensively to the Hall, making it a family home. In October1517, Thomas was granted a licence to export 'wode and billet', made within the lordship of Rochford, in his vessel called the 'Rosendell'.

Today Rochford Hall is the home of the Rochford Hundred Golf Club.

Henry Carey was made a ward of Mary's sister, Anne, upon the death of his father and she oversaw his upbringing. After Anne's execution in 1536, the King assumed the wardship and responsibility of the young Henry Carey. As adults, Catherine and Henry became firm favourites of Elizabeth I who, upon their deaths, had them buried in Westminster Abbey (Catherine in St. Edmund's Chapel and Henry in St. John the Baptist's Chapel).

Henry Carey was created Lord Hunsdon in January 1559 by Elizabeth I. His son George inherited the other moiety (share) of Thomas Boleyn's land from Elizabeth on her death in March 1603.

Mary's second marriage, c.1534, was to William Stafford (b. 1500 d. May 1556), son of Sir Humphrey Stafford. William was a founding member of the Privy Chamber and a soldier who was knighted in Scotland in September 1545. They were married in secret, probably in Calais, and she was pregnant in that year. When this was announced to the family, it resulted in their banishment from court due to misconduct (c. September 1534). He was younger than Mary (aged just 20 to her 34) and a man of lower social standing, but quite possibility the only man willing to marry her. Mary was considered to be spoiled goods after her affairs with the French king and Henry VIII.

William had accompanied Henry VIII and Anne Boleyn to France in 1532 when the King was trying to get public and royal support for the annulment of his marriage to Catherine of Aragon. Mary and Jane, Lady Rochford (her sister-in-law), were in the same group. Later, William provided evidence of Katherine Howard's ill advised affair with Francis Dereham in February 1542 which resulted in her beheading, as well as that of Lady Rochford.

After their banishment, William and Mary lived in relative obscurity for the next six years in Calais, where William is noted as being employed throughout the 1530s. This absence explains why Mary was not involved in the downfalls of Anne and George.

Sources disagree on children from this marriage: one states there was but one child born in nine years while others state there were at least two: Anne (b. c.1535) and Edward (d. c.1543), but neither survived to adulthood.

Mary inherited Rochford Hall upon the death of her grandmother Margaret in March 1540[1], although livery (possession) was not granted until May 1543. One source claims Mary died a 'sudden death' in July 1543[2], aged around 44, but there is no verifiable record of this and her burial place is unknown though St. Peter churchyard, Hever, or St. Andrew church, Rochford, have been suggested. St. Andrew was built by her grandfather, Sir William Boleyn, so it seems a logical place if she died at Rochford. However, the interior memorials show no record of her burial. Her husband William was in France in July 1543, at the head of a hundred foot soldiers, fighting for King Henry. News of his wife's death would not have reached William for some time.

An Inquisition Post Mortem that was performed at Brentwood, dated 4 Apr 1543, has recently come to light which says Mary died on 19 Jul 1543, which is the accepted date by historians. There is obviously a conflict of dates here and it is assumed the Post Mortem date was in error (probably 4 Apr 1544) since she is known to have been alive in May 1543. It also notes the age of her son and heir, Henry: 17 years,15 weeks and 5 days as of 22 Jul 1543.

According to the Patent Rolls of 1539, Mary (then Stafford) was paid a sum of money by King Henry after his purchase of Hever Castle from her uncle, Sir James Boleyn. This was probably another of Henry's quiet efforts to help Mary through her loss of family, home and influence. Henry is rightly characterised as a tyrant but it appears he still felt some responsibility and affection for Mary. It is also recorded that Mary and Henry exchanged New Year's Day gifts in the 1530s and 1540s, a singular honour.

Mary was accorded the title Dame by Henry VIII in Sep 1545, two years after her death when William Stafford was knighted.

---

[1] This is somewhat at odds with Sir William Boleyn's will wherein the hall was bequeathed to Mary's father, Thomas, in 1505. One explanation is that Rochford Hall was given to Margaret upon her marriage to William. Since Thomas died in 1539 it is quite possible Rochford was part of the lands he left Mary and her husband.
[2] Clark, Dr. M., Rochford Hall: The History of a Tudor House.

Anna Bollein Queen.

Anne Boleyn
Drawing by Hans Holbein the Younger
Royal Collection

Chapter 6
Anne Boleyn

Lady Anne Boleyn
Marquess of Pembroke, Queen of England

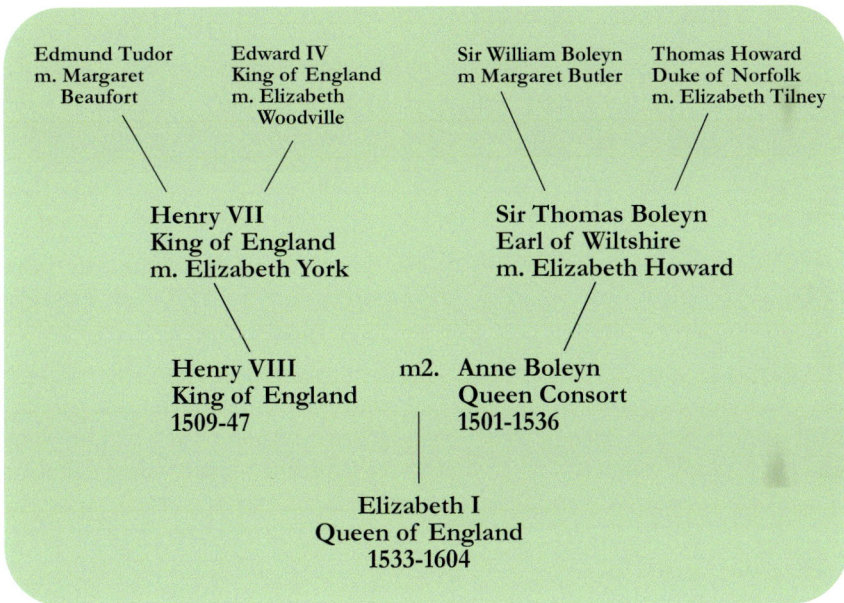

Edmund Tudor m. Margaret Beaufort	Edward IV King of England m. Elizabeth Woodville	Sir William Boleyn m Margaret Butler	Thomas Howard Duke of Norfolk m. Elizabeth Tilney

Henry VII
King of England
m. Elizabeth York

Sir Thomas Boleyn
Earl of Wiltshire
m. Elizabeth Howard

Henry VIII   m2. **Anne Boleyn**
King of England   **Queen Consort**
1509-47   **1501-1536**

Elizabeth I
Queen of England
1533-1604

Anne Boleyn was born c.1501 at Blickling Hall, the daughter of Master Thomas and Lady Elizabeth Boleyn. When she was born she had one older sister, Mary, and probably one older brother, Thomas. Her younger brothers, Henry and George, were born within the next few years. [1]

As a granddaughter of the Duke of Norfolk and the great-granddaughter of the Earl of Ormond, Anne was higher born than Henry VIII's three other English wives. Her early years were spent at Hever where she was prepared by her parents to become a courtier or

---

[1] The exact dates and order of birth of the Boleyn children are unknown, but this is the most likely order and has been assumed throughout this book.

Margaret of Austria

Archduchess Margaret of Austria, Duchess of Savoy, Regent of the Netherlands was the daughter of the Hapsburg Emperor Maximilian I. Her court, at Mechelen (now in Belgium) was considered to be the most prestigious in Europe.

Thomas Boleyn was sent to Margaret's court in 1512 by Henry VIII as a special envoy to negotiate a treaty. He impressed Margaret and was able to arrange for his daughter, Anne, to become one of Margaret's eighteen Maids of Honour.

Margaret was a powerful ruler in her own right, maintaining a period of peace and prosperity in the Netherlands until her death in 1530.

a wife of a prominent nobleman (*'to be at the sharp end of politics, power and profit'* as Ives states it).[1]

In 1513, Anne's father, Sir Thomas, arranged a placement for Anne as one of eighteen maids of honour to the Emperor's daughter, the Archduchess Margaret of Austria, Regent of the Netherlands, at Mechelen (now in Belgium).

This was the most prestigious court in Europe, the premier finishing school, where Anne became fluent in French, learned polished manners and benefited from her mentor Margaret's example.

Accompanied by a Flemish nobleman, Claude Bouton, Anne left England in the summer of 1513 - she would have been 12 or 13 years old.

But in 1514, at the King's request, Anne was withdrawn from Margaret's court and sent to France with Mary Tudor (Henry's sister) who was to marry the elderly French king, Louis XII. However, Louis died less than three months later, and was succeeded by his cousin, Francois I. Anne then joined the court of Francois's wife, the 15 year old Queen Claude.

Anne spent the next seven years at the French court in attendance to Queen Claude and travelled with her to the Field of the Cloth of Gold meeting in June 1520. Was this where Henry VIII first noticed Anne? There is no evidence of this, but it is quite possible that Sir Thomas took this opportunity to introduce his daughter.

Anne was recalled to England at the end of 1521 or early 1522 by her father in anticipation of a marriage to James Butler, son of the 7th Earl of Ormond. She joined Catherine of Aragon's household as the negotiations were conducted. Anne made her debut at court in the company of her sister Mary at the Chateau Vert masque in March 1522 where Anne played the part of Perseverance, Mary played Kindness

[1] Ives E., 2005

and Jane Parker, soon to marry George Boleyn, played Constancy. All were required to speak impeccable French, the language of the cultured court. Anne was not the only Boleyn woman at court: her mother, aunts and sister all served as ladies-in-waiting in the royal household. They all took an oath of loyalty to their royal mistress.

The Ormond estate had been settled upon Sir Thomas Boleyn's mother, Margaret and her sister Anne in 1515, though it was claimed by Piers Butler, who was in occupancy. The idea of the Butler/Boleyn marriage wasn't Sir Thomas's nor Henry's (though he thought it an excellent one). It was a Butler plan, supported by Cardinal Wolsey, to solidify their

Queen Claude of France

Born in 1499, Claude was the eldest daughter of King Louis XII and Duchess Anne of Brittany. At fourteen she was married to her cousin Francois, and they became king and queen on the death of Louis, who had no sons, in 1515.

Claude spent much of her short married life pregnant, having seven children before her death, aged 24 in 1524.

hold over the title and the estate. The proposal came to nothing in the end though the title, Earl of Ormond, was eventually presented to Sir Thomas.

Anne was romantically connected with Henry Percy, 7th Earl of Northumberland (it was believed that there had been an agreement between the two for marriage), and with Thomas Wyatt (the first great Tudor poet) during the period 1522-27. But when Henry VIII, showed an interest in Anne, both suitors wisely gave way.

Anne, George and their father were taken ill by the sweating sickness in June 1528. Henry VIII sent William Butts, his second doctor, to Hever to take care of Anne and her father, whilst George recovered at Waltham Abbey. At the start of the outbreak, Henry fled with Catherine and his daughter Mary to a remote royal house. It was during this time that Anne received seventeen love letters from Henry - the King was in serious pursuit of his next wife.

What was Anne like, you may ask? According to the sources[1], she was captivating to men but not a ravishing beauty, sharp, assertive, subtle, calculating, vindictive, a power dresser and a power player, perhaps a figure to be more admired than liked. She was also highly intelligent, a talented musician (especially the flute), active in field sports and a lover

[1] There are as many opinions of Anne's character and appearance as there are historians who have written about her. Eric Ives, The Life and Death of Anne Boleyn, is probably the most authoritative source, but see the Bibliography at the end of this book for other relevant texts.

and supporter of the arts. Anne became a patron of the painters Hans Holbein the Younger and Lucas Hornebolte (probably recommended by Margaret of Austria where Hornbolte's father was the court painter).

Physically, Anne was tall with long brunette hair and dark eyes, eloquent and gracious. She had a continental style in fashion, manners and dress, easily outshining the other ladies at court.

But Anne had a reputation as a sharp-tongued young woman with a fiery character. She was also known for publicly rebuking her father and even Henry for their timidity, and her uncle, the Duke of Norfolk, for his lack of support. Cardinal Wolsey called her 'the Night Crow'.

Anne became a convinced 'evangelical' with strong religious opinions of her own, seeking reform of the Catholic faith but not its destruction. She was at odds with her parents and her uncle James about these convictions, although her brother George had similar views.

These aspects of Anne's character clearly made her attractive to Henry, but would ultimately contribute to her downfall. Anne's story continues in Chapter 8.

Religion

Anne, her family and their supporters, believed the Catholic Church needed reform, but they were not thinking of destroying it. Even at dinner, they talked about the Bible and religion. There were debates on all points; for example, the King and James Boleyn might join to debate with Hugh Latimer and Nicholas Shaxton.

Anne studied the Bible, especially the French text, but she was a strong supporter of an English version available to the people. Thomas Cromwell was also an advocate (at least privately) of the English Bible, which is perhaps one of the reasons he supported Anne's marriage to Henry, but the Catholic Church saw it as heretical and a threat to their power.

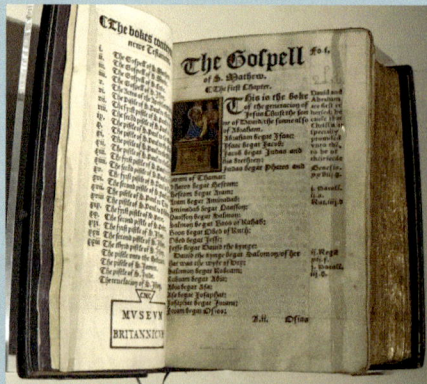

The Tyndale New Testament in the British Library

Anne protected those who were secretly bringing English language Bibles, printed in Germany, into the country in the mid 1530s. She even kept an English version of William Tyndale's New Testament in her Privy Chamber for anyone to read. The Coverdale Bible of 1535 and the Tyndale of 1534 were the primary English versions at the time. Many of the Boleyn religious books ended up in the royal library at Westminster when their property was confiscated by the Crown in 1536.

Chapter 7

George Boleyn and Lady Jane Parker

Sir George Boleyn
Privy Council member, 2nd Viscount Rochford;
and his wife
Lady Jane Parker Boleyn
Viscountess Lady Rochford

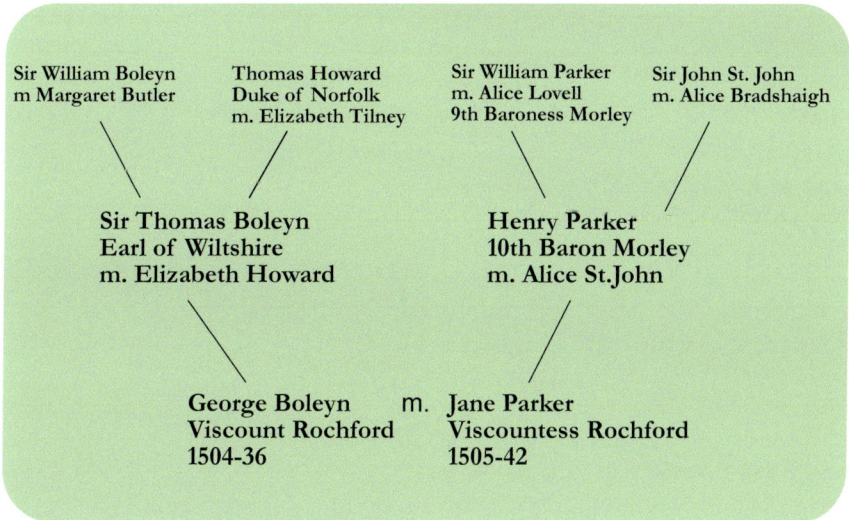

Sir William Boleyn m Margaret Butler	Thomas Howard Duke of Norfolk m. Elizabeth Tilney	Sir William Parker m. Alice Lovell 9th Baroness Morley	Sir John St. John m. Alice Bradshaigh

Sir Thomas Boleyn
Earl of Wiltshire
m. Elizabeth Howard

Henry Parker
10th Baron Morley
m. Alice St.John

George Boleyn   m.   Jane Parker
Viscount Rochford   Viscountess Rochford
1504-36   1505-42

George was very close to his sister Anne and they were together much of the time as they grew up, both educated at home. It is in these siblings that the ambition and intellect of their parents was apparent. Both were exceptional students of language, especially French and Latin. They were brought up to be courtiers, to enter into royal service and thus obtain family and personal wealth and power. This was their parents' goal for them and an accepted vocation for the nobility. George was also particularly adept at archery, bowls and jousting, which made him popular with the King, and he was a voracious reader.

Much of what we know about George comes from the reports of the Imperial Ambassador of Charles V, Eustace Chapuys (a bitter enemy of the Boleyns, prone to inaccurate reporting), the correspondence of

**Portrait of an Unknown Man,
possibly George Boleyn**
Hans Holbein the Younger

the French court, the surviving records of Henry VIII's court and, most damning, information derived from the writings of Boleyn enemies and rivals for power. There was a sustained destruction of anything Boleyn, including paintings and poetry, in the aftermath of the family's fall from grace, all at the orders of the King and conducted by Thomas Cromwell.

George was, like his sister Anne, proud and somewhat arrogant, but he was also charming, intelligent, loyal and he had a more amicable disposition than his tempestuous sister. He was the voice of reason in Anne's more flamboyant moments. He first appeared at court, in an unofficial basis, in 1514-15 when he took part in the Christmas revels.

The poet Thomas Wyatt was one his many friends, but he also acquired many enemies as a result of his intense religious convictions: he was an ardent Reformer with pro-Lutheran opinions. A good deal of this hatred was also due to his closeness to the throne and the resultant power and influence it gave him. His active participation in Henry's divorce of Catherine of Aragon and his subsequent marriage to Anne, made George and the rest of the Boleyns very unpopular. Envy, malice and religious hatred were a potent mixture.

George loved music and poetry and had a genuine, all-consuming interest in theology and the reform of the Catholic church (he was said to have been more Lutheran than Luther). His

The Morleys

Henry Parker, 10th Baron Morley, was a member of the household of Lady Margaret Beaufort (between 1499 and 1509), the mother of Henry VII, and acted as her cupbearer at the coronation feast of Henry VIII. His wife Alice was also part of the Queen's court. He was educated at Oxford and used as a literary translator during Henry's reign. He also served as an ambassador, being one of a party who delivered the Order of the Garter to the Archduke Ferdinand of Austria.

He was present at all the trials for treason of peers during Henry's reign and, in 1536, he sat on the panel which convicted his own son-in-law, George, Viscount Rochford, of treason. To make matters worse, he was present in the Lords for the readings of the bills of attainder which condemned his daughter, Lady Rochford, to death.

Sir Henry had fought on the losing side (for Richard III) at the battle of Bosworth but he was able to work his way back into the good graces of the royal family.

commitment earned him many enemies among those still adhering to Catherine of Aragon and the Catholic faith and this was one of the primary reasons for his fall.

He was fluent in Latin and French as well as being skilled in diplomacy. He is known to have translated, at Anne's request, at least two French religious books into English after she was created Marquess of Pembroke in September 1532.

George Boleyn was born c.1504 at Blickling Hall to Master Thomas and Lady Elizabeth Boleyn, the youngest of five children. His brothers, Thomas and Henry, died in childhood, leaving George and his two older sisters, Mary and Anne. The family moved to Hever Castle, Kent, in early 1506 where he grew up.

Eustace Chapuys

Chapuys was a diplomat from Savoy (now in France, but then part of the Holy Roman Empire) who served Emperor Charles V as his Ambassador to England from 1529 to 1545. In London he lived at Austin Friars within the City walls, a neighbour of Thomas Cromwell, whom he considered a friend. Cromwell and Chapuys found they could be useful to each other.

As a representative of Charles, Chapuys was naturally a strong supporter of Catherine and her daughter, Princess Mary. He was a staunch opponent of France.

His prodigious correspondence with Charles largely survived and has proved of great value to historians and followers of Tudor history. He was popular at Henry's court and picked up gossip and rumour from a network of informants and spies. He never accepted Anne Boleyn as queen, and referred to her in corresponcence disparagingly as 'the Concubine'.

George's first appointment at court was as a Page in the King's Chamber, possibly as early as 1516 at the age of 12. He first appears in official court records in 1522, along with his father, when the King granted them certain offices in Kent. In 1525 Sir Thomas Boleyn arranged a marriage between George and the Honorable Jane Parker, first daughter of Henry Parker, 10th Lord Morley, and Alice St. John.

Jane was born c.1504 in Essex and her early life was spent in the family's manor house, Great Hallingbury, near Bishop's Stortford, and at Fotheringhay, Northamptonshire. She received a very good education and her teenage years were spent at court, where she was to spend much of her life and career. She had at least four siblings: Henry (the heir), Francis, Margaret and Elizabeth. Her father was a classics text translator and an ambassador for both Henry VII and Henry VIII. Her grandfather, Sir William Parker, was Richard III's standard bearer at the Battle of Bosworth Field. But the Parker family were strong supporters of Queen Catherine and her daughter Mary and this caused difficulties for Jane in the following years.

She was first noted at court in June 1520 when she was part of Queen Catherine's party that travelled to Calais, France for the Field of the Cloth of Gold meeting between Henry VIII and Francois I. At this time she was known as 'Mistress Parker' and was one of Catherine's Maids of Honour. Her parents were there, as well as Sir Thomas Boleyn, Lady Elizabeth and Mary Boleyn. Anne Boleyn was there as

Jointures and Dowries

Marriages between wealthy families at this time were more akin to a financial deal between the parents than any kind of love match - the bride and groom would often have had little say in the matter.

The bride's father would have been expected to provide a dowry, an immediate payment of cash to the groom's father, who in turn would be expected to provide a 'jointure' to the couple. The jointure was usually a lifetime interest in land and property which would provide an income for the couple and to the wife in the event her husband pre-deceased her.

There were some variations on this arrangement, particularly for nobility with a title to trade in exchange for money or land from a wealthy, but lower ranked family.

part of the French Queen Claude's household. Mary had recently been married to William Carey who was in attendance as well. It was here that Jane was kissed by the French king during a banquet given by Queen Catherine.

From then on, Jane's life revolved around the glittering court of Henry VIII. Over time, Jane became a Lady In Waiting to queens: Catherine of Aragon, Anne Boleyn, Jane Seymour, Anne of Cleves and finally, Lady of the Privy Chamber to Queen Katherine Howard. She was also a participant in Anne Boleyn's coronation, wearing the new queen's livery of silk and scarlet, which was embroidered with her motto of *"Aisa sera groigne qui groigne"* - i.e. *"Let them grumble, that is how it is going to be"*[1]

In 1521 she saw other side of Henry's court with the execution of the 3rd Duke of Buckingham for treason. He was one of the most powerful nobles in the land and a continuing threat to Henry's claim to the throne. This may well have made her aware that all was not light and joy at Henry's court: there could be danger, intrigue and swift changes in one's position, both good and bad.

In March 1522 she was one of eight ladies who participated in a pageant for the ambassadors of Charles V, the Holy Roman Emperor, at York Place. She was 17, good looking and given a starring role: she had arrived. Her fellow participants included Mary and Anne Boleyn and Mary Tudor, the Dowager French Queen, sister of Henry VIII. It was a mark of her standing in the court. She wore a rich gown of yellow satin, embroidered with her name, (which was among her wardrobe clothing in the 1536 inventory taken upon the death of her husband).

The marriage between George and Jane took place in late 1524 or early 1525 at the parish church of St. Giles, just across the fields from the Parker family home. Henry VIII gave them a wedding present of Grimston Manor in Norfolk.

A pre-nuptial agreement between Sir Thomas Boleyn and Sir Henry Parker covered the financial aspects of the marriage. Jane came with a dowry of 2000 marks (about £1300), which her father would cover. In exchange Sir Thomas guaranteed to convey to her the rents of the

[1] Ives, E. 2005, p.141

manors of Aylesbury and Bierton in Buckinghamshire and various other manors in Norfolk for the rest of her life.

It was an exciting time for Jane as her husband's position within the court rose and Anne's influence grew, but there were times of great stress, fear and turmoil ahead.

George was appointed a Gentleman of the Privy Chamber in 1525, effectively a companion to the King, and then a succession of more senior appointments at court.

In June 1528, George contracted the 'sweating sickness' while with the King and Queen Catherine at Waltham Abbey. His father, Sir Thomas, and his sister, Anne, also contracted the disease but they recovered at Hever Castle while George recovered at the Abbey.

In October 1529, George was knighted, and made 2nd Viscount Rochford in December upon his father being created Earl of Wiltshire (Rochford being part of Sir Thomas's estate at the time). Jane became Viscountess Lady Rochford.

Now, at 25, he undertook the first of six diplomatic assignments to France as an ambassador. He quickly established a good relationship with King Francois I of France.

His mission was to encourage the French universities to support Henry VIII's divorce from Catherine. In two following missions, both in 1533, he succeeded in getting Francois to once again support Henry with the Pope. However, by this time the Pope had already excommunicated Henry (15 July 1533).

In the early 1530s George and Jane were allowed the Palace of Beaulieu (New Hall), the King's house, as their chief residence after the banishment of Henry's daughter Princess Mary to Hatfield Palace. George would have spent much time at court and on the King's business between 1530 and 1536, but Jane less so. She developed a close relationship with Anne both before and after her marriage to Henry but was dismissed from the court in the autumn of 1534 when she

Palace of Beaulieu

The estate of New Hall (north-east of Chelmsford in Essex) was granted to Thomas Butler, 7th Earl of Ormonde in 1471 and inherited by Margaret Butler, Thomas Boleyn's mother, on his death in 1515.

Thomas sold the estate to Henry VIII in 1516 for £1000 and the King rebuilt the house in brick. He gave his new palace the name Beaulieu, meaning 'beautiful place' in French. George Boleyn was appointed 'keeper' of the palace, and Henry and his court spent over a month there in July 1527.

The palace still stands and is now used as an independent school.

conspired against a young woman of Anne's court whom the King had been accustomed to serve. This was done at the queen's request after she noticed a supporter of Princess Mary had become another of Henry's many mistresses. Jane was not supported by Anne nor anyone else in the Boleyn faction/family when the King had her banished for meddling in his affairs.

The evidence suggests Jane lived at Blickling Hall until her return to court in late 1536, after the trial of her husband George, as all her 'stuff' was still there when she was arrested in 1541. *'Parcelles of Stuff that did remain a chest beyng in the chambr over the kechen'.*[1] The rooms above the Tudor kitchens in Blickling's West Wing were bedrooms although the quote may refer to Grimston Manor, another of the Rochfords' houses.

George's achievements illustrate Henry's trust and regard for him, and point out how extreme Henry's later actions were. It seems unlikely that Henry believed the charges brought against George. He was, however, quite willing to turn his back on George, as he had done with other close members of the court.

There are suggestions that George and Jane's relationship was not romantic - a marriage of convenience - George being labelled as 'promiscuous' and there being no known children. However, it is generally assumed that they were estranged by late 1535 though they exchanged letters whenever George was out of the country on diplomatic missions. If estranged, this could be due, in part, to George's intense evangelical beliefs, which Jane would have found difficult to accept as she, and her family, were of the old conservative religion. Her father, Lord Morley, was a strong supporter of Queen Catherine and Princess Mary and it appears Jane leaned that way as well.

Jane had to legally battle her father-in-law, Thomas Boleyn, to receive her jointure in its entirety. Apparently, Thomas also treated his daughter Mary in the same manner after the death of her first husband, William Carey, but ended up granting her much of the Boleyn wealth in his will. He eventually gave Jane the manors specified, which included the Blickling estate, upon being pressured by Henry and Cromwell.

[1] Taff J., Courting Scandal p.134

Chapter 8
Henry VIII and Anne Boleyn

By 1526 Henry VIII had already taken Mary Boleyn as a mistress, and was becoming interested in her younger sister, Anne. But he was still married to Catherine of Aragon.

Henry's rejection of Catherine had begun in 1524 when he gave up sleeping with her, having no hope of a son. He was 30 and she was 39 and had not conceived in seven years. Henry began thinking of a new marriage.

However, in June 1525, Henry made his illegitimate son, Henry Fitzroy (b. 1519, d July 1536), the Duke of Richmond and Somerset giving him precedence over everyone, even Henry's legitimate daughter Mary.

Fitzroy was the son of Bessie Blount, one of Catherine's maids of honour and one of Henry's many mistresses. Henry's intent may have been to make Fitzroy his heir, but this was a risky option opposed by many in the court. Henry was convinced to seek an annulment of his marriage instead, based on religious grounds: that she had been the wife of his brother Arthur, which made the marriage invalid in canon law. Fitzroy was to later marry Mary Howard, a cousin of Anne Boleyn, but he died of tubercolosis in 1536 at St. James Palace.

By May 1527 Henry took the first steps to divorce Catherine. Anne doesn't appear as a love interest

Henry VIII, c.1531
Joos van Cleeve, Royal Collection

The Embassies

There were three principal embassies in England during Anne's time: Venice, France and the Holy Roman Empire (which comprised much of central Europe that is now Germany, Switzerland, Austria and northern Italy).

The objective of the French was to keep Henry VIII from allying with Charles V, the emperor, who had a chronic rivalry with France. Charles also had a family interest in his Catholic aunt, Queen Catherine.

Charles' ambassador was Eustace Chapuys, a lawyer from Savoy, who arrived in England in 1529, staying until 1545. He became the focus for those who disliked what was going on, especially Anne's enemies. France hoped to benefit from her known love of the country, its culture and its language.

until the early part of 1526 and then only as a possible mistress. Anne submitted to Henry's advances in January 1527 but only as a potential wife. In August 1527, Henry applied to the pope (Clement VII) for a dispensation to allow him to marry again.

According to Chapuys,[1] Sir Thomas Boleyn, Anne's father, did try to dissuade Henry from the marriage:

"I must add that the said Earl of Wiltshire has never declared himself up to this moment; on the contrary, he has hitherto, as the Duke of Norfolk has frequently told me, tried to dissuade the King rather than otherwise from the marriage."

Between December 1527 and October 1528, there was an outbreak of the sweating sickness and Anne and Sir Thomas went to Hever to recover. Henry wrote 17 love letters to Anne: ten in French, the rest in English. None are dated and Anne kept them at Hever. However, they were either stolen from Anne or 'lost' shortly after the death of Sir Thomas in 1539, resurfacing in the Vatican in the 17th century. The most likely explanation is that Archbishop Cranmer slipped them out of England after Sir Thomas's death to prevent them falling into the hands of Cromwell and the King.

When the pope failed to support Henry's divorce, Anne introduced Henry to Dr. Thomas Cranmer of Jesus College, Cambridge, a renowned theologian and a Boleyn supporter. Cranmer told Henry he didn't need the decision of canon law for his divorce: theologians would give him the answer. Henry could then bypass the papal curia and the pope, giving the decision to the doctors of the Church. Anne was also instrumental in Henry's decision as she had been providing him with books that argued that kings were appointed by God and therefore not accountable to popes. Tyndale's English version of The Obedience of a Christian Man was one of these.

In October 1529, Henry accepted Cranmer's option and tasked him to present a thesis to the theologians of France and Italy. Both Sir

---

[1] Despatches of Eustace Chapuys, 15 Feb 1533 (written after the marriage had taken place, although Chapuys was not aware of it).

Thomas and his son, George, were deeply involved in this effort with Sir Thomas escorting Cranmer to Italy in January 1530.

There were several factions at work in Henry's court at this time. They included the Boleyns, the conservatives, who supported Queen Catherine and Princess Mary, the Seymours who sought to replace Anne with Jane and then there were those supporting Cromwell.

Direct opposition to the King's will was impossible – it would have been considered treason and led to the Tower. The loyal way to compete for benefit and for authority over policy was to seek Henry's favour. Henry's will remained dominant; when he decided, that was final. But he was vulnerable to all the factions around him and could be manipulated.

Anne's faction included Thomas Cromwell (initially, but he was to become the man most responsible for her downfall), Thomas Cranmer (who was also a supporter of the Boleyn's program of religious reform), Edward Fox (a firebrand on the divorce issue) and, of course, her brother George.

Her enemies (other factions) included, to name a few, the Duke and Duchess of Norfolk (her uncle and aunt), Nicholas Carew (a king's favourite and a cousin of Anne who would become prominent in her downfall), the Duke of Suffolk (an opponent of the divorce), Henry Guildford (controller of the household and strong supporter of Queen Catherine), and Reginald Pole (the King's cousin who saw the divorce as a possible threat to the succession as well as doing economic damage to vital trade routes).

In 1531, Cromwell, now one of Cranmer's counsellors, began to help in the divorce battle. He produced draft legislation to enable the divorce to be granted by the English Church instead of the pope. When there arose great opposition to this, Cromwell convinced the King to declare himself Supreme Head of the Church....all other options were thrown aside. When the clergy showed signs of fighting this too, Cromwell produced a bill to strip the church of its powers and Henry took this to parliament and within a few days, it was approved. Also in the summer of 1531, Henry dismissed Catherine from the court.

Two books provided by Anne and George were prominent in Henry's decision to declare

Anne's Charity

During her time as queen, Anne gave standing orders for the relief of the deserving poor and the prompt handling of petitioners. She increased the purses of the royal maundy, sewed clothes with her ladies to be distributed to the poor when on progresses and ensured pregnant women received sheets and two shillings. She even supported legislation on poverty, which Henry himself brought and introduced to the Commons on 11 March 1536 and pledged to contribute to the act's costs. She also supported education and scholarship.

Her women at court received regular wages and livery and were entitled to free food and accommodation.

himself as the Supreme Head of the Church of England: *The Obedience of the Christian Man* (1528 William Tyndale), which demonstrated the political expression of royal authority: 'One king, one law is God's ordinance in every realm', and *Doctor and Student* (1531 Christopher St. German) which suggested that Parliament had the power to regulate all the actions of the Church in the temporal sphere. They basically said Henry could achieve his divorce by parliamentary authority and that, as a sovereign ruler, he was also the head of the church.

On 1st September 1532, at Windsor Castle, Anne was created Marquess of Pembroke in her own right. She was given precedence over all other peers, apart from the three dukes (Norfolk, Suffolk and Buckingham), thus becoming superior in rank to her own father. Anne was also given a patent granting lands worth £1000 a year. This was done in advance of Henry and Anne's meeting with Francois I at Calais in October. Anne was to be presented as the next Queen of England and she needed status and European acclaim. This included her jewellery - she had a pendant designed by Hans Holbein with the initials 'H' and 'A' intertwined and a brooch with 'RA', Regina Anna, in diamonds.

Both the King's sister, Mary Tudor Brandon, and Elizabeth Howard, the Duchess of Norfolk, refused to attend the Calais meeting, as did the French king's sister, Margaret of Navarre, but Anne's sister Mary and sister-in-law Jane, Lady Rochford, were in attendance. It is widely believed that Anne and Henry consummated their formal commitment to marry during this trip.

Anne and Henry had a secret wedding ceremony on 25 January 1533 in the upper chamber over the Holbein Gate of Whitehall, at dawn, with few witnesses. Anne's parents and brother, Henry Norris, William Brereton, Thomas Heneage (the latter two of the Privy chamber) and Lady Berkeley are known to have been there. Dr Roland Lee, Bishop of Coventry and Litchfield, presided. The marriage was probably driven by Anne's pregnancy; Henry wanted to make sure their child was seen as being a legitimate heir. It was at this point that Anne adopted the phrase 'the Most Happy'. The wedding was legitimised the next day by parliament under Cromwell's direction. By March, an

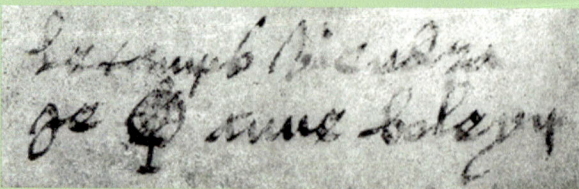

From Anne's Book of Hours, now at Hever Castle
The armillary sphere, drawn by her (a symbol of constancy), can be matched with her motto (adopted later by her daughter Elizabeth I):
'Semper eadem', meaning 'Always the same'.

announcement was being carried to Francois I by Lord Rochford (Anne's brother George) that they were married and she was pregnant. Most of the court, including the foreign ambassadors, didn't know about the marriage until March or April.

Thomas Cranmer was made Archbishop of Canterbury on 30 March 1533 and shortly thereafter both parliament and the English church convocation gave their support for Henry's divorce and marriage to Anne. However, Henry continued negotiating with the papal authorities about his marriage. Some two years later (April 1535) Cromwell is noted as communicating with a papal envoy in order to seek Pope Paul III's approval for Henry's divorce and marriage.

Now officially married, Anne was given the regal honours of Queen during Easter, 12th April, 1533 and she was given all the estates and houses previously belonging to Queen Catherine. Her household was sworn in, including her uncle James Boleyn, now her chancellor. However, opposition to the marriage and the radical religious changes continued from such persons as the Duke of Norfolk, Henry's sister Mary and her husband, the Duke of Suffolk. Mary adamantly refused to accept her brother's choice of wife up to her death on 24th June 1533.

Anne's coronation was on Whit Sunday, 1st June, 1533.

The pageantry was spread over four days, the last being the actual coronation ceremony in Westminster Abbey where she sat in Edward I's chair and was anointed by Archbishop Cranmer with St. Edward's crown. Over 800 people attended the following feast. Only the Queen and archbishop sat at the top table - the King sat in a box overlooking the hall. The Queen was presented with 28 dishes for the first course, then 24 for the second and 30 for the third.[1] Eighteen Knights of the Bath and fifty Knights Bachelor were created during this period, many of them being Boleyn supporters, including Cromwell, Norris, Brereton, Henry Parker, brother of Jane Boleyn, and Francis Weston. Several would lose their lives on the scaffold in 1536, accused of being Anne's lovers.

Anne was blamed by all and sundry for the breakup of Henry's marriage to Catherine, for the establishment of the Protestant religion in England and for any other disruption that occurred… plague, famine, uprisings, etc. etc. Her treatment of Catherine and Mary (the future 'Bloody Mary') brought discontent within both the court and with the public. However, much of the hostility to Anne was due to a dislike of Henry's policies… she was the convenient target. A majority of what we know about this discontent comes from Cromwell's records. He had his finger firmly on the public and court pulse.

---

[1] Ives, E. 2005, p.225

ANNA BOLINA · ANG · RECINA

Anne Boleyn, artist unknown, late-16th century
There are several versions of this painting including one at Hever Castle and
one in the National Portrait Gallery, London, made after her death, possibly
copies of a contemporary painting that no longer survives.

Chapter 9
Downfall

The birth of a daughter, Elizabeth (named after her two grandmothers), on 7th September 1533 was a disappointment for both Henry and Anne but it was not the 'crushing psychological blow' that is often stated. Henry was actually relieved that it was a safe delivery. Heralds were widely sent to proclaim the birth, choristers sang at the Chapel Royal and letters were sent far and wide announcing it, including to the French king and to Emperor Charles V. The Archbishop of Canterbury, Thomas Cranmer, was made Elizabeth's godfather.

However, it did weaken Anne's claim to the throne as she had not produced the hoped-for son. To make the situation more stressful, in March 1534 the Pope declared Henry's marriage to Catherine of Aragon lawful. By July 1534 Anne was pregnant again but, unfortunately, she miscarried. Still, Henry continued to proclaim his love for Anne.

In both 1533 and 1534, Henry was publicly taken to task by Anne for having mistresses during her period of pregnancies: Catherine looked the other way but Anne and her notoriously fiery temper didn't. According to Chapuys, Henry responded by saying

> 'she must shut her eyes, and endure as well as more worthy persons, and that she ought to know that it was in his power to humble her again in a moment more than he had exalted her'. [1]

He was not enthralled with her anymore. In September 1534 Chapuys reported:

> "the King has been very sad, and has sent [his mistress] a message to this effect: that she ought to be satisfied with what he had done for her; for, were he to commence again, he would certainly not do as much; she ought to consider where she came from" [2]

During their summer progress (a royal tour around the country) of September 1535, Henry and Anne stopped at Wolf Hall, Wiltshire, for a week's stay. The hall was the home of Sir John Seymour and his

[1] CSPS Vol. 4 Part 2, 1531-1533, pp.787-800: 3 Sept. 1533
[2] CSPS Vol. 5 Part 1, 1534-35:, pp.252-267: 23 Sept. 1534

family. This included the elder daughter, Jane, who nine months later would become Henry's third queen. Previous to this, Jane had served both Catherine of Aragon and Anne as a lady-in-waiting.

Meanwhile Cromwell was considering doing a deal with Charles V as a foil against France. According to a source, Henry knew of this and encouraged Cromwell to proceed. It appears Anne was also aware of these negotiations but was firmly opposed to any deal that would hinder Elizabeth's title to the throne, including restoring Princess Mary as heir.

Then there was Charles' reluctance to come to any terms as long as Anne usurped his aunt's place as queen. This problem was temporarily resolved on the 7th January 1536 when Catherine, aged 51, died at Kimbolton Castle (her tomb is in Peterborough Cathedral). Her death brought relief to the court and enthusiasm for the Boleyn marriage, but it also removed a safeguard of Anne's position. It left her exposed to the fluctuations of Henry's conscience. With Catherine's death, there was no reason for further enmity or possible war with Charles V.

Evidence points to February 1536 as the beginning of Henry's serious interest in Jane Seymour and Chapuys was reporting that Henry was contemplating a third marriage. By then, Anne was sure that she was pregnant again, but she knew of her husband's interest in Jane.

On 24th January 1536, Henry's horse fell heavily in the tiltyard at Greenwich and rolled over him, knocking him unconscious for two hours. Henry was a big man and was wearing about a hundredweight of armour (approximately 50kg). Add to that the size of his horse and its armour and you can see how serious the incident was. Present medical opinion suggests this could have caused some brain damage resulting in a change in personality.

Five days later, on the 29th January, Anne miscarried a son (ironically on the day of Catherine of Aragon's funeral). Henry was said to have not been himself, disoriented since the fall, then the miscarriage. He was very upset, saying at one point, 'I see that God will not give me male children'. But he did not accuse Anne of failure, nor did he take any steps to replace her. In fact, he was still making determined efforts to persuade Europe to accept her as his legitimate wife as late as 30th April. However, he continued his affair with Jane Seymour.

Anne's miscarriage was not her last chance nor the point at which Jane Seymour replaced her in Henry's priorities. However, she was still without the all-important son. Her enemies now believed they could unseat her by convincing the King that a new, uncontested, marriage was the answer. Nicholas Carew, a one-time ally of Anne's, was the leader of this effort, with the support of the Boleyn opponents in the privy chamber. But it was the argument with Cromwell that kickstarted the effort to remove Anne.

In late March 1536, Anne and Cromwell had a major argument in which she said she would like to see *'his head off his shoulders'*. A major cause was his legislation, the Dissolution Act, to confiscate the wealth of the monasteries. Anne, and other prominent reformers, including Cranmer, wished the funds to be applied to education and other charitable causes. Cromwell, however, wanted the wealth to go to the King to help solve his financial problems and make Henry the richest prince in Christendom. It would also dramatically increase Cromwell's influence and power (and wealth). Henry enthusiastically supported this and made sure the Commons

Thomas Cromwell 1485-1540
Hans Hobein the Younger,

concurred. It was at this point that Cromwell began shifting his allegiance from Anne to Jane. Cromwell's suppression of approximately 376 monasteries by 1536 brought over £132,000[1] to the royal treasury and gave Cromwell a great deal of influence over the King

On the **1st April 1536**, in conversation with Chapuys, Cromwell let slip that he was not in alliance with Anne and suggested he had not supported her marriage to Henry though, in fact, he had worked very hard to see it happen.

On Sunday **2nd April**, a few days after the Cromwell argument, and with Anne's apparent approval, both Henry and Cromwell were roundly criticised by her almoner, John Skip, in his Sunday mass for their actions concerning the monasteries. Both were livid and the story quickly spread through the court. Cromwell did try to moderate the Dissolution Act to appease the queen but Henry gave that short shrift. Henry was to later tell Jane Seymour *'not to meddle in state affairs like the last queen had, as she died in consequence'*. Another reason for Anne's fall.

Throughout April 1536, Jane, her family and their conservative supporters made subtle efforts to convince Henry that it was time to divorce Anne and marry Jane. The evidence suggests that Henry was not averse to this advice. However, there is nothing in the sources that

---

[1] £132,000 would be worth something like £91million today, but compared to the size of the British economy at the time, it would have a similar impact to £44 billion Source https://www.measuringworth.com/

indicates that Anne's enemies sought her death - divorce or annulment was their plan. It would be Cromwell and Henry who sealed her fate.

By the middle of April, Anne had become a major threat to Cromwell: her influence with Henry could easily result in his fall and his allies were few. He decided to undermine the King's confidence in Anne to ensure his own power would remain unchallenged and help outmanoeuvre and dominate whatever factions formed around the King after her removal. The initial plan was to rid himself of Anne first, with the support of Princess Mary and her allies, and then neutralise them too.

Within days, he had the support for Henry to divorce Anne and marry Jane Seymour from Nicholas Carew, the Seymours, then Jane herself and Princess Mary. But Cromwell knew that if Henry just divorced Anne and sent her to a convent, it would not ensure his survival. He had to confront Henry with evidence that would force the King into rejecting Anne permanently. Cromwell needed a capital charge, one that would convince Henry that she was guilty.

Cromwell used the informal and playful aspects of Anne's court to build a case of adultery and incest. Her brother George and men of the King's Privy Chamber – Francis Weston, William Brereton, Henry Norris ('gentle Mr Norris' as he was known at court), and Mark Smeaton – were framed as her accomplices and co-conspirators. Naming people who were in close proximity emphasised the existential danger to the King.

Knowing very well that accusations of the queen's sexual relations with others at court would trigger Henry's hatred, deep worries about the legitimacy of his children and his longing for a male heir, it was a short step to turn flirtatious familiarity around Anne into a sinister plot to end his life. The plan was guaranteed to arouse the worst elements of Henry's characteristics of pride, quick anger, suspicion and paranoia.

Chapuys admitted that he helped Cromwell plan Anne's downfall at Princess Mary's request:

> *"I have since employed various means for the accomplishment of the said affair, sometimes talking about it to Master Cromwell, and to such others as seemed to me most fit for the purpose."*[1]

Monday 24th April. Henry approved the setting up of a commission by Cromwell to investigate certain cases of treason in Middlesex and Kent. Cromwell needed to act quickly to keep any of the accused from using their personal influence with Henry. With the commission at hand, prosecution could proceed immediately upon their arrest. He didn't want the King to have second thoughts once this broke.

Tuesday 25th April. Henry sent a letter to his ambassador in Rome (Richard Pate) in which he referred to the 'likelihood and appearance that God will send us heirs male' and described Anne as 'our most dear

---

[1] CSPS Vol.5 Part 2, 1536-1538, pp.104-118: 2 May 1536

and most entirely beloved wife and queen'. Copies were also sent to his ambassadors in Paris.

Thursday 27th April. Cromwell sent out writs to summon an emergency sitting of Parliament, ostensibly to plan negotiations with Charles V. Henry gave his approval, unaware that Cromwell was plotting to rid himself of the Queen.

Saturday, 29th April. Cromwell thought he had the perfect opportunity when he was told of a furious dispute between Anne and Henry Norris about his supposed feelings for her. Anne was reported to have said, *"You look for dead men's shoes. For if aught came to the King but good, you would look to have me."*[1] A further argument occurred the next day between Anne and Henry VIII over this, but it appears she and Norris were able to convince the King that there was nothing to it. But Henry remained suspicious, and this is when Cromwell made Henry aware of the overall accusations against Anne and her co-conspirators. Henry didn't believe them but he told Cromwell to investigate. Cromwell still needed a trigger to jolt the King into unthinking action.

In the meantime, Cromwell was digging for incriminating evidence to help build his case. The first of these was a deathbed confession by Bridget, Lady Wingfield, a longtime friend of Anne's, concerning a comment Anne had made in a letter about an 'indiscreet trouble'. Lady Wingfield thought it meant a lack of moral authority, possibly a sexual relationship between Anne and Lord Percy as part of a verbal agreement between the two to be married. Anne always denied it but the suspicion was there. How this got to Cromwell is not known but it is believed it was via the Duke of Suffolk. A note written by John Spelman, one of the judges at the trials of Anne and George, said it was Lady Wingfield who provided the main accusation.

Other court ladies were sources of information. These included Anne Cobham and Elizabeth Somerset, the Countess of Worcester, (whose brother, Sir Anthony Browne, was a great supporter of Princess Mary and a member of the privy chamber) plus 'one maid more' (possibly Margery Horsman). Lady Worcester and Margery Horsman were close friends of the queen. Cromwell's version of events was crafted around Lady Worcester's comments to her brother that the queen had 'offended' (meaning she had had a sexual relationship) with both Smeaton and her brother George.

Cromwell's interrogations of Jane, Lady Rochford, only provided gossip and hearsay, and there is nothing that indicates Jane's testimony was ever used. Anne was supposed to have confided in Jane about the King's sexual problems and she then told George. Jane is accused of telling Cromwell this but there is no surviving contemporaneous document that backs it up.

---

[1] This story was recorded in letters, since lost in a fire, used in a work by John Strype according to Ives. E. (2005), p335

Cromwell, at this point, believed he had all the evidence he needed to condemn Anne and George.

Sunday, 30th April saw the arrest of the first suspect, Mark Smeaton, a musician in Anne's court, and a commoner (though made a Groom of the Privy Chamber in 1532). He had been overheard telling Anne about his feelings for her and his desire to be accepted as a courtier. He was quickly brought to Cromwell's house in Stepney, interrogated and accused of adultery with the queen. He was sent to the Tower in irons, the only one of the accused to receive this treatment. There he confessed (probably after being tortured on the rack) to having been Anne's lover. Smeaton was the only commoner - the other five accused were gentlemen and therefore not subjected to torture.

Monday, 1st May 1536. The May Day jousts at Greenwich went ahead with Henry, Anne and the Boleyns in attendance (George was one of the jousters). Cromwell chose this moment to tell Henry about Smeaton's confession. The King immediately left the joust on horseback with Norris in tow, and never saw Anne again.

Norris was the closest friend Henry had, but having been reminded by Cromwell of Norris's conversation with Anne, Henry interrogated him on the way, offering a pardon if he would admit adultery with the queen. Norris insisted on his innocence and was sent to the Tower early the next day.

Cromwell now had the ammunition to destroy the Queen, Norris and George Boleyn. Norris, although he gave a confession, withdrew it the next day, claiming he had been duped by William FitzWilliam. Henry expressed his grief, hurt and anger by spilling copious tears at the same time as defaming Anne with increasingly wild accusations.

Later that morning, at Greenwich, the queen was summoned to appear before the King's Council where she was accused of adultery with five men, arrested, and taken by boat to the Tower, about 5pm, to be held in the Lieutenant's Apartments - a house within the walls of the Tower, now known as the Queen's House.

Sir William Kingston, Constable of the Tower, reported to Cromwell that upon her arrival, Anne was weeping and laughing on her knees claiming her innocence. It was seen as a nervous collapse. At this point, she only knew of Norris and Smeaton's arrest. Anne was placed with a number of unsympathetic attendants who were to report everything she said. She later wrote:

> *'I think it much unkindness in the King to put such about me as I never loved…. I would have had those of mine own privy chamber which I favour most'.*

Her attendants were: Lady Kingston, wife of the Tower's Constable and a supporter of Princess Mary, Margaret Cosyns (or Coffin), Lady Elizabeth Wood Boleyn, Anne's aunt and wife of Sir James Boleyn, and Margaret Stonor. Margaret Cosyns in particular spied on Anne and reported her words to both Kingston and Chapuys.

Cromwell deliberately chose women known to be loyal to Queen Catherine and Princess Mary and hostile to Anne. But the women who initially despised Anne when they first joined her in the Tower came to care for her deeply.

Tuesday, 2nd May. George Boleyn (Viscount Rochford), was arrested at Whitehall, whilst attempting to see the King after having heard of his sister's arrest. Cromwell was wary of George's influence with Henry and had him arrested and imprisoned in the Martin Tower of the Tower of London. Even Cranmer was blocked from seeing the King.

Anne and George's estates were seized by the Crown upon their arrests. Competition within the court for this bonanza of titles, land and wealth was intense.

Wednesday, 3rd May. Archbishop Cranmer wrote a letter to the King trying to intercede on Anne's behalf. It was supportive:

> *"I never had better opinion of in woman, than I had in her; which maketh me to think she should not be culpable"*

But cautious:

> *"I think your highness would not have gone so far, except she had surely been culpable ... your grace knoweth best".[1]*

Thursday 4th May and **Friday 5th May**. Sir Richard Page, Sir Thomas Wyatt, Sir Francis Weston, Sir William Brereton and Francis Bryan (Anne's cousin) were summoned, questioned by Cromwell, and sent to the Tower. Only Weston was not a Boleyn supporter. Cromwell selected these men as part of his plan to eliminate the Boleyn faction, especially in the Privy Chamber. Brereton was arrested because of his opposition to Cromwell's policies in Wales. Sir Thomas and Lady Elizabeth Boleyn were not arrested or questioned.

George was charged with having had sexual relations with his sister at Westminster on 5th November 1535, but records show Anne was with Henry at Windsor Castle on that day. This is a prime example of the fabricated charges that were used to convict Anne, George and the others.

The King granted Jane Rochford permission to send a message to her husband in which she told him she would attempt to intervene with the King on his behalf. The note was delivered to George by two Boleyn arch enemies, Sir Nicholas Carew (later beheaded for treason in 1539) and Sir Francis Bryan. Jane, however, did not approach the King, for fear of drawing unwelcome attention to herself.

---

[1] Originally from Burnet G *The History of the Reformation of the Church of England*, 1865, reproduced in Norton, E. (2011)

Saturday, 6th May. Anne wrote to Henry proclaiming her innocence and begging for his forgiveness. A copy was found amongst Cromwell's papers, endorsed 'To the King from the Lady in the Tower', in his handwriting.[1] The letter shows that she understood exactly what was going on, that this was a plot by her enemies and that Henry's affections now lay elsewhere:

> *"whose name I could some good while since, have pointed unto; your grace being not ignorant of my suspicion".*

She pleaded:

> *"let me have a lawful trial, and let not my sworn enemies sit as my accusers and my judges".[2]*

Tuesday 9th May. Juries were empanelled and indictments produced.

Wednesday 10th May. Giles Heron, foreman of the Grand Jury of Middlesex and son-in-law of the late Sir Thomas More, announced that the jury had decided that there was sufficient evidence to suggest that Anne Boleyn, George Boleyn, Mark Smeaton, Sir Henry Norris, Sir Francis Weston and Sir William Brereton were guilty of the alleged crimes and should go to trial.

Friday 12th May. Weston, Norris, Brereton and Smeaton were brought to Westminster Hall for their trial. They knew their fate was sealed when they saw the jurymen. Cromwell had selected a very hostile panel, most of whom were beholden to him or supporters of Princess Mary, but it also included Sir Thomas Boleyn. Only Smeaton had confessed, the rest pleaded not guilty. They had no advance warning of the charges, couldn't call witnesses and had no defence counsel. The expected verdict came.

GUILTY!

They were sentenced to be hung, drawn and quartered.

Chapuys:

> *"only the last-named [Smeaton] confessed having slept with the concubine [Anne][3] on three different occasions; all the others were sentenced on mere presumption or on very slight grounds, without legal proof or valid confession."[4]*

All of the condemned were allowed to write farewell letters to their families, but only Francis Weston's has survived.

---

[1] Any letter from the prisoners would have been passed to Cromwell by Sir William Kingston, the Constable of the Tower. Cromwell clearly made a copy of the letter himself before passing it on to the King – if indeed it ever was shown to the King.

[2] Norton, E. 2011

[3] In his letters, Chapuys usually referred to Anne as 'the concubine'. As a supporter of Queen Catherine and Princess Mary (Catherine was a cousin of his master, Charles V) Chapuys refused to recognise the marriage of Anne to Henry.

[4] CSPS Vol. 5 Part 2, pp.118-133: 19 May 1536

Saturday 13th May. Anne Boleyn's household was broken up.

Monday 15th May. On the second floor of the White Tower, adjoining the chapel of St. John, benches and seats were made for the approximately two thousand spectators where Anne was to stand trial. Thomas Howard, the Duke of Norfolk sat as Lord Steward, holding his white staff of office; his son, Henry Howard, the Earl of Surrey, sat at his feet holding the golden staff of office as Earl Marshall; and twenty-six peers acted as the jury. Norfolk was a self-serving opportunist who always adapted to the King's wishes and he knew the result the King wanted, even though Anne was his niece (Anne's mother, Elizabeth Howard Boleyn, was the Duke of Norfolk's sister).

Anne put on a confident and assured display and received much sympathy from the audience during her trial. She knew she would have great difficulty establishing her innocence with the jury selected by Cromwell. The verdict was a foregone conclusion: her supposed lovers had been found guilty a few days earlier. Norfolk pronounced the judgement:

GUILTY!

And sentenced her to burning on Tower Green or 'have thy head smitten off' – the choice left to the King's pleasure.

Chapuys described Anne's reaction:

> *"When the sentence was read to her, she received it quite calmly, and said that she was prepared to die, but was extremely sorry to hear that others, who were innocent and the King's loyal subjects, should share her fate and die through her. She ended by begging that some time should be allowed for her to prepare her soul for death."* [1]

He also reported that Henry told Jane Seymour on the morning of the trial that Anne would be condemned by three in the afternoon.

Almost all of the Crown's allegations of repeated adultery by Anne between October 1533 and December 1535 can now be disproved, including Smeaton's. One modern legal opinion even states that they were 'immaterial' in that having intercourse with a queen who consented was no crime in common law at the time. [2]

Shortly after Anne's trial, that of George, Viscount Rochford, began. Same day, same place, same jury minus one peer: Henry Percy, 6th Earl of Northumberland, the man Anne had been brought back from France to marry, *"was suddenly taken ill"* [3]. George pleaded not guilty and, like his sister, made an impressive defence which in any other

---

[1] CSPS Vol. 5 Part 2, pp.118-133: 19 May 1536

[2] Margery S. Schauer and Frederick Schauer, Law as the Engine of State: The Trial of Anne Boleyn, 22 Wm. & Mary L. Rev. 49 (1980), https://scholarship.law.wm.edu/wmlr/vol22/iss1/3

[3] LP Vol. 10, January-June 1536: 15 May 1536

circumstances would have destroyed the prosecution's case. Chapuys reported:

> *"no proof of his guilt was produced except that of his having once passed many hours in her company, and other little follies. He answered so well that many who were present at the trial, and heard what he said, had no difficulty in waging* [betting] *two to one that he would be acquitted, the more so that no witnesses were called to give evidence against him or against her, as is customary in such cases".*

But George himself sealed his own fate when he read aloud from the note Cromwell handed to him that spoke of the King's sexual difficulties or, more significantly, the accusation of Elizabeth Browne, Countess of Worcester. Either one would have been enough to see him declared guilty in this biased court.

Once again, Norfolk pronounced judgement against one of his sister's children.

GUILTY!

George accepted his fate and his only thought was for those he owed money - he even read out a list of his debts before leaving the court. Back in the Tower, he asked for the privilege of access to the eucharist before he died, a powerful assertion of innocence.

Tuesday 16th May. Archbishop Thomas Cranmer, at Henry's direction, visited Anne in the Tower to act as her confessor. Some say that he was primarily sent to try to get her consent to an annulment of her marriage to Henry.

Sir William Kingston wrote to Cromwell reporting: "*Yet this day at dinner the Queen said she would go to anonre* [a nunnery] *and is in hope of life*". This implies Anne believed, that by agreeing her marriage to Henry was null and void, she would be spared the death sentence and allowed to lead the rest of her life in peace.

Wednesday 17th May. Cranmer declared the marriage between Henry and Anne null and void. No public justification was made.

On the same day, George Boleyn was led to the scaffold on Tower Hill. Chapuys reported:

> *"before dying [he] declared himself to be innocent of all the charges brought against him, though he owned that he deserved death for having been contaminated with the new heresies, and having caused many others to be infected with them. He had no doubt, said he on the scaffold, that God had punished him for that"* [1]

The executioner, with one stroke of the axe, and in front of a crowd of approximately two thousand onlookers, ended the life of Anne's thirty-two year old brother.

---

[1] CSPS Vol. 5 Part 2, pp.118-133: 19 May 1536

Norris, Brereton, Weston and Smeaton were executed after him (all by axe, their sentences having been commuted to beheading instead of being hanged, drawn and quartered), Smeaton being the last. Only he had confessed and it is suggested that he had been savagely tortured on the rack. He did not take the opportunity to retract his confession on the scaffold. When told of this, Anne is recorded as saying *'did he not exonerate me, before he died, of the public infamy he laid on me? Alas! I fear his soul will suffer for it'* [1] None of the men's heads were put on display on spikes, the usual routine with convicted traitors.

George was buried in the chancel area of the Chapel of St. Peter ad Vincula within the Tower. The other four were buried in two graves in the churchyard: Henry Norris and William Brereton in one, and Francis Weston shared his final resting place with Mark Smeaton.

Thursday 18th May. Anne summoned Kingston to hear mass with her. She then swore on the sacrament that she had never been unfaithful to the King; she did this twice. A powerful statement of innocence. It was considered instant damnation to lie on the Body of Christ and when word spread of what Anne had done, it went far to rehabilitate her reputation. Nobody believed a woman due to meet her maker would damn her immortal soul by lying on the Host.

Chapuys reported:

"The lady in whose keeping she has been sends me word, in great secrecy, that before and after her receiving the Holy Sacrament, she affirmed, on peril of her soul's damnation, that she had not misconducted herself so far as her husband the King was concerned."[2]

Friday 19th May 1536. The Tower of London.

Anne was to be beheaded by an expert French swordsman, known as the 'Sword of Calais'. This was Henry's 'gift of mercy' to her. His name was Jean Rombaud and he was paid £23 – approximately £7,500 in today's money. As the Spanish Chronicle stated Henry VIII sent for the swordsman before Anne was even put on trial:

"He had sent a week before to St. Omer for a headsman who could cut off the head with a sword instead of an axe, and nine days after they sent he arrived". [3]

A passage recently found in a Tudor warrant book in the National Archives describes Henry's precise instructions to Kingston about how Anne should die. Henry made clear his desire to be rid of the *"late queen of England, lately our wife, recently attainted and convicted of high treason"*[4] and as an act of mercy decreed that she should be spared burning at

---

[1] LP Vol. 10, pp424-440, 2nd June 1536
[2] CSPS Vol. 5 Part 2, pp.118-133: 19 May 1536
[3] Norton, E. 2011, p.225. The 'Spanish Chronicle' was written by an unknown Spanish merchant residing in London, and is unreliable. The headsman is often said to have come from Calais, and it is more likely that this was arranged by Cromwell.
[4] Cunningham, S., 2020, quoting the King's writ for the execution.

the stake saying: *"we, however, command that…the head of the same Anne shall be….cut off."*

A little before noon on the 19th May, a crowd of over a thousand gathered on what is now the parade ground north of the White Tower. Amongst the spectators were the Dukes of Norfolk and Suffolk, earls, nobles and lords, the Mayor of London with aldermen and sheriffs, along with representatives of the guilds, the Lord Chancellor Thomas Audley, Thomas Cromwell and his son Gregory, and other members of the King's council. Henry's illegitimate son, Henry Fitzroy, Duke of Richmond and Somerset, was there as his father's witness, with his friend the Earl of Surrey. Fitzroy had been on the jury that condemned Anne and George.

Anne, in company with her ladies, Kingston and a large contingent of soldiers, walked through the crowd to the scaffold. As was customary, she was given the opportunity to make a last speech:

> *"Good Christian people, I am come hither to die, for according to the law and by the law I am judged to die, and therefore I will speak nothing against it. I am come hither to accuse no man, nor to speak anything of that whereof I am accused and condemned to die, but I pray God save the King and send him long to reign over you, for a gentler nor a more merciful prince was there never: and to me he was ever a good, a gentle, and sovereign lord. And if any person will meddle of my cause, I require them to judge the best. And thus I take my leave of the world and of you all, and I heartily desire you all to pray for me."[1]*

At the scaffold, having made her speech, Anne removed the ermine mantle to reveal her slender neck to the executioner. She kept glancing behind her, fearing he would strike before she was ready and perhaps hoping for a last minute reprieve. She knelt, with her head bowed, and began to pray. Then something remarkable happened. One by one, the thousand onlookers dropped to their knees on the grass and joined her in prayer, many openly wept. Only Fitzroy and Charles Brandon remained standing, likely staring around with incredulity at what was happening.

In the midst of her prayers, the executioner swung his sword and the deed was done.

One of Anne's ladies covered her head while the others covered her body and carried them to the nearby chapel, passing the two recently filled graves of her supposed lovers. It is now believed that the 'young' ladies who accompanied Anne to the scaffold were her own ladies from the court and not Cromwell's. They cried so hard at Anne's beheading that one witness said they seemed "bereft of souls". They

---

[1] Several versions of this speech were recorded. This is an extract from John Foxe's *Actes and Monuments*, reproduced in Grueninger N., 2022 and also in Norton E., *2011.*

ended up risking the King's rage to make sure Anne's remains were treated with respect.

Her clothes were removed and given to the Tower as part of their rights, the Crown paying Kingston £100 for them and Anne's jewellery. Her corpse was then put in an elm arrow chest (no proper coffin having been provided) and buried unceremoniously in the chancel of the Tower's Chapel Royal of St. Peter ad Vincula, to the right of the altar, near her brother.

On hearing confirmation of Anne's death, Henry immediately rode to see Jane Seymour who was with her family in a house close by.

The day after Anne's execution, Henry VIII and Jane Seymour were engaged.

It wasn't long afterward that Cromwell proceeded against the Seymours but that's another story. Cromwell was himself struck down four years later.

The Earl of Wiltshire, Sir Thomas Boleyn and his wife, Lady Elizabeth had both returned to Hever in Kent when Anne was arrested, although Sir Thomas was in London for the trials of the Weston, Norris, Brereton and Smeaton on the 12th of May. On 19th June 1536, Thomas turned over the Privy Seal to the King, who shortly thereafter gave it to Thomas Cromwell.

Thomas Wyatt, a supporter of Anne and a love interest, had been arrested but not charged. He watched the executions of Anne's supposed lovers and her brother from the Bell Tower. His reaction to these executions was reflected in his later poetry:

"These bloody days have broken my heart.
My lust, my youth did them depart
And blind desire of estate.
Who hastes to climb seeks to revert.
Of truth, circa Regna tonat"[1]

This poem is often known by its refrain 'circa Regna tonat' which translates *'Around the throne, thunder rolls'*.

He was released in the summer of 1536 and is reported to have never fully recovered from those scenes. He had been accused of supplying damaging information during his interrogation and received a £100 payment later that month. *'I was made a filling instrument/ to frame other, while I was beguiled'*. Wyatt's poem is in the Devonshire Manuscript. [2]

To illustrate how the verdicts of those condemned were foregone conclusions, inventories of the estates and belongings of all the accused were prepared well before their trials. There was an undignified

[1] Norton E.2011

[2] Heale E. The Devonshire Manuscript was originally compiled by Margaret Douglas, Countess of Lennox and contained court poetry by Thomas Wyatt and others.

scramble for the lands and offices of the accused, their estates being distributed before they had even faced a jury, and many of those who received a share then sat on the juries that condemned them.

"No English Queen has made more impact on the history of the nation than Anne Boleyn, and few have been so persistently maligned."
Joanna Denny

"A bold, high-spirited and independent woman, she had played politics for high stakes, not as an agent but as a principal. In doing so, she had used the weapons with which nature had endowed her: wit, charm, intelligence … Cruel and unjust as her fate may now appear, she suffered the standard penalty at the time for being a dangerous loser. In that sense her execution was in itself a tribute to her power."
Professor David Loades

"Intelligence, spirit and courage"
Thomas Cromwell

Chapter 10
The Aftermath

Sir Thomas and Lady Elizabeth Boleyn

The Earl of Wiltshire, Sir Thomas Boleyn and his wife, Lady Elizabeth both returned to Hever in Kent when Anne was arrested, although Sir Thomas was in London for the trials of Weston, Norris, Brereton and Smeaton on the 12th of May. On 19th June 1536, Sir Thomas turned over the Privy Seal to the King, who shortly thereafter gave it to Thomas Cromwell.

By May 1536, when George and Anne were arrested and imprisoned in the Tower, Elizabeth and Thomas were in no doubt that their family's grip on power was very much in danger. They were most likely aware of the enquiries being conducted by Thomas Cromwell's commissioners, at Henry's insistence, though they may not have been aware of the actual accusations. There is nothing to indicate Lady Elizabeth or Sir Thomas were personally interrogated by Cromwell or his assistants during collection of evidence against Queen Anne.

Neither parent was allowed (by the King's command) to communicate with or visit their children in the Tower of London, and an intervention with Henry was impossible. The King would not have agreed to see them and they would have faced possible arrest, capital punishment for defying the pre-ordained verdict. Henry had already made up his mind and moved on. Cromwell and the juries knew what the verdicts had to be. It was dangerous to question the King's decision, especially in such a serious matter.

Sir Thomas sat on the trial of the other accused men (Mark Smeaton, Henry Norris, Sir Francis Weston and William Brereton) but not on George or Anne's. By the time of their trials, Elizabeth and Thomas had already left London, seeking solace at Hever Castle.

Their worst fears were realised when told of the beheading of George, by axe, on 17th May 1536 and then Anne, by sword, on the 19th. Who told them the sad news is unknown, but it is quite possible it was Archbishop Cranmer, who was a close friend of the family. He had attempted to intervene on their behalf with the King, but Cromwell had made sure that did not happen.

Lady Elizabeth and Sir Thomas were not completely isolated from the King and the court afterwards. In October 1536, Sir Thomas was ordered by Henry to raise troops to counter a rebellion in Lincolnshire and Yorkshire (the Pilgrimage of Grace). Lady Elizabeth's presence at the court was noted in June 1537 when Lady Lisle's agent sought her advice on a question of etiquette. They both attended Prince Edward's christening on 15 October 1537 and were once again at court in January 1538.

Lady Elizabeth died on 3 April 1538 in a house near Baynard's Castle, the home of the Abbot of Reading in the City of London, and was buried in the Howard chapel, St. Mary-at-Lambeth (now deconsecrated and housing the Garden Museum). It was noted as early as April 1536 that she was suffering from a severe cough 'which grieves her sore', quite possibly tuberculosis, which was common at the time.

Sir Thomas died at Hever on 12th or 13th March 1539 and was buried in St. Peter's Church, next to the castle. His steward, Robert Cranewell, sent a short note to Cromwell telling him of the death. Henry spent £16 on masses for Thomas' soul and Parliament collected another £200 (approx. £60,000 in today's money) for more masses.

Thomas Cromwell's letter for the seizure of Sir Thomas's papers was received at Hever on 26th March, some two weeks after Sir Thomas's death. The old house must have been partially emptied, as Sir John Tebold wrote to Thomas Cromwell that

> *"much of the goods in the manor house at Hever have been removed by the advice of the Archbishop of Canterbury; part of the stuff and all the implements yet remain. I have stayed them by the advice of Sir Thomas Willoughby till the King's further pleasure".*[1]

This could explain why Henry's love letters to Anne were found in the Vatican Library in Rome. Cranmer may have sent much of the Boleyn paperwork there as a safe-guard from the King and Cromwell who, most likely, would have destroyed them, as they did with any Boleyn items they came across after the family's downfall.

Lady Margaret Butler Boleyn

Lady Margaret Butler Boleyn, mother of Sir Thomas and widow of Sir William Boleyn, continued to live at Hever until her death c.March 1540 (the date is not definite) some time after Thomas who had died at Hever in March 1539. She was approximately 90 years old and was buried in St. Peter's churchyard, next to Hever Castle, the same church where Thomas was buried.

Between March 1539, when Thomas died, and her own death, Margaret was probably taken care of by her remaining family (sons James and/or Edward though there is presently no confirmation of them being there) and her Hever servants. There are notations of a John Tebold of Seal, Thomas's man in Kent, being in charge at Hever

[1] LP Vol. 14 Part 1, pp.239-264: 26 March 1539

at the time. He coordinated with Sir Thomas Willoughby *"in entertaining the old Lady Boleyn there in best wise to her comfort"*. Willoughby had notified Thomas Cromwell, the King's Secretary, of the situation and it is believed the King let her live there until her end. Margaret's granddaughter, Mary Boleyn, was in Calais with her husband, William Stafford, who was serving in the army.

Lady Margaret outlived most of the family: her husband William, son Thomas, his wife Elizabeth, granddaughter Anne and grandson George. Only her daughter, Anne Boleyn Shelton (the eldest surviving child), sons William, James and Edward and granddaughter Mary survived her. Mary and her husband William later claimed Margaret's Butler lands.

Mary Boleyn Stafford

Mary had been in Calais with her husband William Stafford when Anne and George were executed and so escaped any involvement. She inherited Rochford Hall upon the death of her grandmother Margaret in March 1540[1], although livery (possession) was not granted until May 1543. There is little recorded about Mary after Anne's death until her own in 1543, probably at Rochford Hall while her husband was in France fighting for King Henry.

Lady Jane Rochford

After George Boleyn's execution, his wife, Jane, Lady Rochford, spent some time at Blickling. Now out of favour at Court she relied upon the jointure, agreed by her father and Sir Thomas Boleyn, which made provision for her needs in the event of her husband's demise. This included the Blickling estate. Jane lived in Norfolk, staying either at Blickling or at Grimston Manor, from 1534 until late 1536 when she was permitted to return to court (she found living in the country too quiet).

Cromwell's plan had always been to destroy the Boleyn supremacy, which he achieved through the deaths of Anne and George, but he had no issues with Jane at this time. He facilitated her return and received Henry's approval for her to retain her title as Lady Rochford. It is probable that Jane acted as a 'spy' for Cromwell in her position within the queen's Privy Chamber.

She quickly re-immersed herself in court life. She became Lady of the Bedchamber to Queen Jane Seymour in 1536 and she, her father and her brother Henry, were among the chief mourners at Queen Jane's funeral in October 1537. In August 1540, she became Lady of the

---

[1] This is somewhat at odds with Sir William Boleyn's will wherein the hall was bequeathed to Mary's father, Thomas, in 1505. One explanation is that Rochford Hall was given to Margaret upon her marriage to William. Since Thomas died in 1539 it is quite possible Rochford was part of the lands he left Mary and her husband.

Privy Chamber to Queen Katherine Howard. This would eventually prove her undoing.

By late 1541, she had become involved in Katherine Howard's affair with Thomas Culpeper. Reports by the Queen's servants to Archbishop Cranmer resulted in Katherine and Lady Rochford being arrested in November 1541 on the charge of treason and taken to the Tower. The servants' evidence made it clear that Lady Rochford had arranged private meetings for Katherine and Culpeper. There was no firm evidence that the couple did anything more serious than talk, but Katherine's case was undermined by proven pre-marital 'romps'.

After several months of interrogation in the Tower, Jane was showing symptons of madness.[1] This was reported to Henry who then sent his own doctor to retore her but she remained terrified. Wanting another quick ending to this scandal, Henry had an Act of Attainder passed by Parliament on 6th February 1542 wherein Katherine Howard and Lady Rochford were sentenced to death without a trial. Henry also had an act approved which would allow the execution of the insane, just in case.

Lady Rochford was beheaded by axe at 9am on 13th February 1542 at Tower Green, aged about 36, immediately after Katherine, on the same block, which was still wet with the queen's blood. They were buried unceremoniously in the Tower's Chapel Royal, next to each other. Today there are plaques to each in the chapel floor, in front of the altar. Jane died unliked and unlamented.

An inventory taken on 11th November 1541 of Lady Rochford's possessions in the Palace of Westminster consisted mostly of clothing, jewellery and several silver flagons. Almost all her garments were black, as was appropriate for a widow.

More of Jane's belongings, or 'stuff' as the Privy Council described it, were found at Blickling and given to Sir James Boleyn in February 1542 when he inherited the estate.

---

[1] Taffe, J., p.193. If she had 'lost her mind' she could not be legally executed.

Chapter 11

The Other Boleyns

Sir Thomas Boleyn had three younger brothers and four sisters who survived into adulthood, all of whom were the children of Sir William Boleyn and Lady Margaret Butler Boleyn. They play only minor parts in this story, but they were all born at Blickling, and several are buried at Blickling.

Sir James Boleyn

James was born at Blickling c.1480. He married Elizabeth Wode, or Wood (b. c.1480) sometime before 1512. She was one of four daughters (the other three being Alice, Anne and Dorothy) of John Wode (d. c.1496) and his wife, Margaret, of East Barsham, Norfolk, who also had a son, Roger, born around 1492. There were no known children from the marriage of James and Elizabeth. Elizabeth Wode's sister Anne died in childbirth at Blickling on 18 August 1512 during a visit, having given birth unexpectedly to twins, a boy and a girl. They are all buried in Blickling church. Elizabeth's brother Roger died on pilgrimage to Jerusalem in 1518.

Known as Lady Boleyn at court, Elizabeth served Queen Anne Boleyn during her imprisonment in the Tower and may have accompanied Anne to her beheading. Apparently, Anne and Elizabeth didn't get along, which may explain why Elizabeth was not a member of Anne's household though she was at court. She was, however, one of the Ladies at Table for Queen Catherine of Aragon (July 1517). The date of her death is unknown, although she almost certainly died before her husband.

James was knighted prior to December 1516 by Henry VIII as Sir James Boleyn, Knight of Blickling and Salle, aged approximately 36. He lived mainly in Norfolk.

Sir James was a Justice of the Peace for Norfolk from 1511 until his death in 1561 and was very involved with local politics. He sat as MP for Norfolk in 1529 and possibly in 1536. He was also Chancellor of the Household for his niece Anne Boleyn 1533-36 and Knight of the Body for Henry VIII c. 1533. He did not suffer from the fall of the Queen and her brother. He is noted in the records as owing Queen Anne £50 at the time of her death. He attended the 3rd Duke of

Norfolk at the reception of Anne of Cleves in January 1540. Otherwise, he retired from court to his home in Norfolk.

He served as *custos rotulorum* ("keeper of the rolls") for Norfolk from 1558-60.

Sir James succeeded to the entailed lands of his elder brother, Thomas, shortly after Sir Thomas's death in 1539. This included Hever Castle where their mother, Lady Margaret Butler Boleyn, continued to live until her death in 1539/40. James then sold the castle by indenture to the King for £200 on 31 December 1539/40.

In the 1540's and 1550's James consolidated his holdings in Norfolk, exchanging his brother's lands in Kent with the King for grants of monastic land in the Blickling area (especially the bishops of Norwich manor at Blickling, bringing the two halves of the original manor back together). The Boleyn half had originally been willed to Sir Thomas by his father, Sir William, in 1505. Sir Thomas then assigned it to Jane, Lady Rochford, as part of her marriage jointure. She held a 'life interest' in the estate. When she was beheaded in 1542, the estate reverted to Sir James, the next Boleyn male heir. He was the last Boleyn to live at Blickling.

In 1558, on her accession, his great-niece Elizabeth I acknowledged his position, confirming him in his title to his estates and the manors of Blickling, Stiffkey, Filby, Postwick and others.

Sir James died in December 1561 and was buried with great pomp in the family vault in Blickling church. In his will (20 August 1561, titled as Sir James Bowleyne of Blicklyn[1]), he left the Queen a basin and gilt ewer, his written book of the revelations of Saint Bridget and a moiety, or share, of his estate, which included part of Blickling. She, in turn, granted parts of this moiety to the rising lawyer, Henry Hobart of Intwood, in the early 1600s.

James also stated in his will that his great-nephew Edward Clere Esq., the grandson of his sister Alice, owed him £400. This was part of the debt Edward's father John incurred when he purchased the Manor of Blickling from Sir James in 1553. Where Sir James lived from 1553 until his death in 1561/62 is uncertain. It may have been at Mulbarton, one of the Boleyn manors, or he may have continued to live at Blickling.

The Norwich Heritage Centre has recently discovered that a Wycliffe Bible in their collection belonged to Sir James.[2] It is possible he was given this Bible by his niece, Anne Boleyn, as the first English language Bibles came in from Europe in c.1535 through her efforts. They weren't printed in England until 1537 onwards. She kept one on a podium in her private rooms for anyone to read.

---

[1] National Archives ref. PROB-11-44-387
[2] Eastern Daily Press, 19th April 2018.

William Boleyn, Archdeacon of Winchester Cathedral

William was born at Blickling c.1491, the last surviving son of Sir William and Lady Margaret.

His career was primarily the clergy. He achieved the degrees of a Bachelor of Arts in 1503-4 and Master of Arts in 1507. He was a university preacher at Cambridge in 1511, a Prebendary of St. Pauls 1516-17, a Rector of St. Peters, Cheapside, London (1517-29), a Rector of Holt and Postwick and appointed the Archdeacon of Winchester Cathedral (1530-1551) by Thomas Wolsey[1], at the behest of Henry VIII who, at the time, was trying to win the affections of William's niece, Anne Boleyn.

In later years William lived at Stiffkey Manor in Norfolk, which was owned by the Boleyn family. He died without issue in October 1571 and was buried at St. John's church in the village on 6 February 1552 (listed in the parish records as William Bulleyn).

Sir Edward Boleyn

Edward was born at Blickling, c.1495/6, to Sir William and Lady Margaret and was probably the youngest of their children.

Edward married (c.1516) Lady Anne Agnes Tempest (1506- c.1536), of Bracewell Hall, Yorkshire, daughter and coheir, with sister Margaret, of Sir John Tempest and his wife Joan. The Tempest family were an old, prominent family in Yorkshire and strong supporters of Henry V and Henry VI.

Anne and Edward had four daughters and one son: Elizabeth (b. 1520), Mary (1516), Ursula (1518), Amy (or Anne, 1522) and Edward (c.1531, son and heir). Edward was listed as a Suffolk representative as 'Sir Edward Boleyn' at the Field of the Cloth of Gold meeting in June 1520. Lady Anne came into her Yorkshire inheritance when her father died in November 1520.

Lady Anne was an aunt to Anne Boleyn and, as Lady Boleyn, was also at the Field of Cloth of Gold as a favoured attendant of Queen Catherine of Aragon. In 1517 she stood proxy for Mary Tudor, Henry VIII's sister, at the christening at Hatfield Palace of Mary's daughter Frances.

Edward spent most of his time at his wife's estates in Yorkshire having inherited, in right of his wife, Houghton and Medley manors in November 1520.

Edward died on 18 December 1571 and is recorded as being buried in the family crypt in Blickling church.

---

[1] An entry in the Bishop's Register for Thomas Wolsey as the Bishop of Winchester, in 1530 included the appointment of William Boleyn as Archdeacon of Winchester on 20 January.

The Boleyn Sisters

The sisters of Sir Thomas Boleyn, the daughters of Sir William Boleyn and Lady Margaret, were not often mentioned in the records of the day. They were born and lived at Blickling and were just as important, in their own way, as their brothers. They were raised for marriage and they all married into prominent Norfolk families.

Anne, Lady Shelton, b.c.1483

There were two sisters named Anne. The first, born 1475 died at the age of 3 and is buried at Blickling. The second was born in 1483 and should not be confused with Sir Thomas's daughter Anne who went on to marry Henry VIII.

Anne married Sir John Shelton (1472-1539), 21st Lord Shelton, Knight of the Bath, Justice of the Peace, and High Sheriff of Norfolk and Suffolk in Blickling Hall in 1512. They settled at Shelton Hall, in South Norfolk. There are fine stained glass windows of the couple in Shelton church.

Sir John was appointed by Queen Anne Boleyn as the steward of the joint household of Henry VIII's daughters, Mary and Elizabeth. Lady Shelton was appointed as a governess of Princess Mary, which is believed to have been a great burden on her. She was summoned several times by the Duke of Norfolk, Sir Thomas Boleyn and George Boleyn because she had been treating Mary with 'too great kindness and regard'. Mary reciprocated the kindness when she became Queen, sending gifts to the Sheltons on New Year's Day. In December 1556 Mary settled a yearly annuity on Lady Shelton after Sir John's death. She was also granted the manor of Rollesby, Norfolk. Princess Elizabeth spent considerable time at Shelton Hall when she was growing up.

Lady Anne and Sir John had ten known children, including Sir John (the heir, later 22nd Lord Shelton, who married Margaret Parker, sister of Jane, Lady Rochford), Ralph, Thomas, Amy, Anne, Elizabeth, Emma, Gabrielle (a nun of Barking and living in Carrow Priory near Norwich in 1536), Margaret and Mary (1518-1570).

Their daughter Mary, first cousin to Anne Boleyn, is thought to have been a mistress of Henry VIII for about 6 months in 1535.

Mary Lady Heveningham

Hans Hobein, Royal Collection

She was part of Queen Anne's household, functioning as a Maid of Honour, and was part of Anne's Coronation Procession.

Mary was also a major contributor to the Devonshire Manuscript, a collection of 185 poems and jottings that circulated among the young male and female courtiers, including the poet Thomas Wyatt. She later married Sir Anthony Heveningham c.1546. Her portrait was painted by Hans Holbein The Younger.

Lady Anne Shelton was one of those appointed by Cromwell to stay with Queen Anne while she was held in the Tower of London before her trial and execution. She died on 6th January 1556 and is buried either at St. Mary's, Shelton along with her husband or possibly at Carrow Abbey.

Jane, Lady Calthorpe, b.c.1485

Jane Boleyn, who was also sometimes known as Amata or Amy, was born at Blickling in 1485. She married Sir Philip Calthorpe (1480-April 1549) of Ewerton Hall, Suffolk in November 1518.

They had one child, a daughter named Elizabeth (1521-May 1578), who married Sir Henry Parker, Knight of the Bath, son and heir to the 10th Lord Morley, and sister of Jane Rochford. They had one son, Philip.

Anne Boleyn, the future Queen, visited Ewerton Hall on several occasions before her marriage to Henry VIII, as did her daughter Elizabeth I.

In 1521, when Princess Mary was five years old, Lady Calthorpe replaced Lady Bryan as her governess and Sir Phillip was put in charge of the household at joint wages of £40 per annum. In 1525, when Mary set up her household at Ludlow Castle as Princess of Wales, Sir Philip was her vice-chamberlain and Lady Calthorpe was one of her gentlewomen. Mary sent the Calthorpes a New Year's gift in 1542/3.

Lady Calthorpe died in 1543 and is believed to have been buried in St. Andrew's church, Norwich. Sir Philip is buried in St. Mary's Church, Ewerton.

Alice, Lady Clere, b.c.1487

Alice Boleyn was born at Blickling c.1487. She married Sir Robert Clere (c.1453-August 1529), Justice of the Peace and Sheriff of Norfolk and Suffolk, as his second wife in January 1506 after the death of his first wife, Anna Hopton, the previous year. Alice's father bequeathed her £330 upon her marriage.

Robert was knighted in 1494 by the future Henry VIII. Their children included John (Admiral Sir John Clere MP), Richard (died young), Thomas and Edward. It was Sir John who bought the Blickling estate from Sir James Boleyn in 1553. In October 1560, the estate was granted to Sir John's son, Sir Edward Clere, MP.

Lady Alice and Sir Robert attended upon Queen Catherine at the Field of the Cloth of Gold. In 1533, Lady Alice and her sister Lady Anne Shelton were appointed by their niece, Queen Anne Boleyn, as the chief female officers of the household of Henry VIII's daughter, Princess Mary. Alice was considered the kinder of the two. She was also a senior member of Princess Elizabeth's household while she was living at Hatfield Palace.

Lady Alice received twenty manors as her jointure, including the marital home at Ormesby, upon Sir Robert's death in 1529. She also received a house in Norwich, all of which made her a wealthy widow.

Alice died on 1st November 1538 and is buried in St. Margaret's churchyard, Ormesby St. Margaret with her husband. Her will left the Clere's wealth and estate to her eldest son John.

Margaret, Lady Sackville, b.c.1489

Margaret Boleyn was born at Blickling c.1489. She was married in 1506, at the age of 17, to Sir John Sackville of Buckhurst (1483-1557), MP, Justice of the Peace and Sheriff of Sussex and Surrey. They had three sons (Sir Richard MP, Christopher MP and John MP) and three daughters (Isabel, Anne and Mary).

Apart from sharing with his brother-in-law, Sir Thomas Boleyn, in the presentation to a prebend of St. Stephen's chapel, Westminster, Sir John derived no lasting benefit from his Boleyn marriage, having done little on his own account to augment his inheritance. He was Lord of Bergholt, Sackville and Buckhurst from 1524 to 1557. Lady Margaret was primarily involved in educating and preparing her children for their roles in society.

Margaret and John passed their closing years at Chiddingly, Sussex, one of their manors. Lady Margaret died c.1550 and is believed to have been buried with her husband in the Sackville chantry chapel at Withyham, Sussex. However, this chapel, its bells, tombs and register were all destroyed by a lightning strike in 1663.

Chapter 12

Elizabeth

Princess Elizabeth Tudor,
daughter of Henry VIII and Anne Boleyn,
later to become
Queen Elizabeth I of England

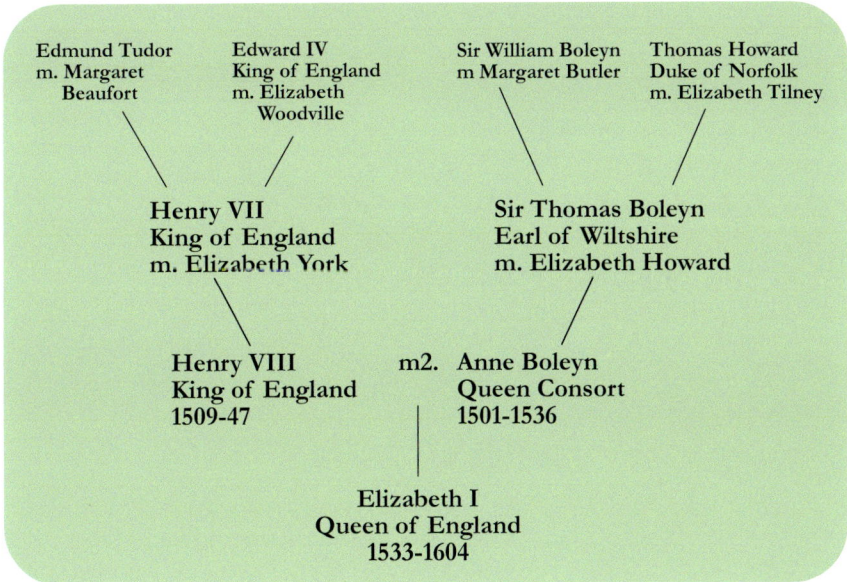

Edmund Tudor m. Margaret Beaufort	Edward IV King of England m. Elizabeth Woodville	Sir William Boleyn m Margaret Butler	Thomas Howard Duke of Norfolk m. Elizabeth Tilney

Henry VII
King of England
m. Elizabeth York

Sir Thomas Boleyn
Earl of Wiltshire
m. Elizabeth Howard

Henry VIII
King of England
1509-47

m2. **Anne Boleyn**
Queen Consort
1501-1536

Elizabeth I
Queen of England
1533-1604

Elizabeth was born on 7 September 1533 at the Palace of Placentia, Greenwich and was named after her grandmothers, Elizabeth of York and Lady Elizabeth Howard. She was their only surviving child. She was baptised on 10 September 1533 and her godparents included Thomas Cranmer, Archbishop of Canterbury; Elizabeth Stafford, Duchess of Norfolk; and Henry Courtenay, Marquess of Exeter. Her uncle, George Boleyn, Viscount Rochford, helped carried a canopy over her at the ceremony.

By the age of two years and eight months, her parents marriage had been annulled, her mother was executed and Elizabeth was declared

Elizabeth I when a Princess
Oil on oanel, painted for Henry VIII by William Scrots
Royal Collection

illegitimate and deprived of her place in the royal succession[1]. Henry married Jane Seymour 11 days after Anne's execution.

In 1537, Jane gave birth to a son, Edward, but suffered in childbirth and died shortly after. As was the custom, Edward was sent to live at Hatfield Palace, and Elizabeth, now almost 7, was placed in his

---

[1] Henry VIII's second Act of Succession. The first declared Mary illegitimate when he divorced Catherone of Aragon.

household and carried the baptismal cloth at his christening. Edward was the undisputed heir apparent to the throne.

Elizabeth's governesses, Margaret Bryan and Catherine "Kat" Champernowne, were instrumental in her upbringing and education. Champernowne taught Elizabeth four languages: French, Dutch, Italian and Spanish. By 1544, when a tutor, William Grindal, was assigned, Elizabeth could write in English, Latin and Italian. Under him she progressed in French and even Greek. By the age of 12 she was translating her stepmother Catherine Parr's religious works into Latin and French. Throughout her life she continued to translate works of the classical authors, including Tacitus and Cicero. By the time her formal education ended in 1550, she was considered one of the best educated women of her generation. She was also proficient in spoken languages including Welsh, Cornish, Scottish, Irish as well as English.

In 1543 Henry had a change of heart and passed the third Act of Succession which declared that, should Edward die without heirs, Mary and Elizabeth would succeed in turn. He confirmed this in his will of 1546 and added the offspring of his younger sister Mary and her husband the Duke of Suffolk to the line.

Henry, died in 1547 and Edward became king at the age of nine. During his reign England was governed by a regency council led by Edward Seymour, Duke of Somerset, Edward's uncle and oldest brother of Jane Seymour.

Henry's widow, Catherine Parr then married her true love, Thomas Seymour, the younger brother of Jane. The Seymours took Elizabeth into their household at Chelsea, but her experiences during this period may have affected her attitude to men for the rest of her life. It is suggested that Thomas engaged her in 'horseplay' (she was only 12 at the time) as well as making 'unwelcome' morning visits to her bedroom. Catherine was to end this after finding them in an embrace[1].

Thomas continued his scheming to gain control of Elizabeth, more so after the

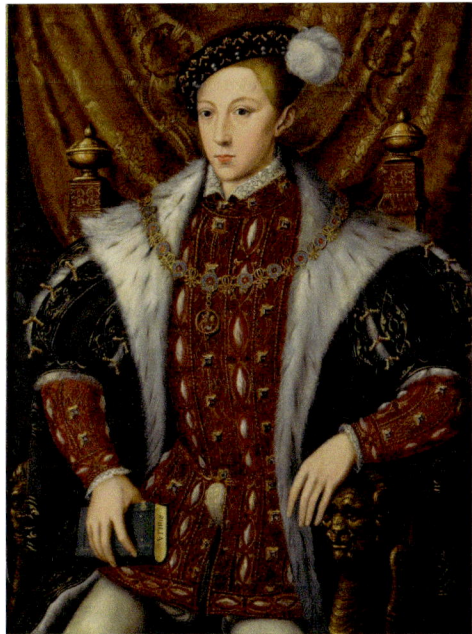

Edward VI
Oil on panel, circle of William Scrots, privately owned.

[1] Borman T., 2024

death of his wife in September 1548. This all ended upon Seymour's arrest and imprisonment in January 1549 charged with conspiring to depose his brother Somerset as Protector and take Elizabeth as his wife. He was beheaded on 20 March 1549.

Edward VI died on 6 July 1553, aged 15, probably from tuberculosis. His will for the succession ignored the Act of 1543, excluded both Mary and Elizabeth, and instead named Lady Jane Grey (granddaughter of Mary Tudor, Henry VIII's sister), as his successor. Nine days later she was deposed by Mary, who entered into London on 3 August 1553 with Elizabeth at her side and took the throne as Mary I.

This sisterly solidarity didn't last long as Mary, a devout Catholic, was determined to eliminate the Protestant faith, ordering everyone to attend Catholic Mass, including Elizabeth. She had to outwardly conform, becoming a focal point for the country's discontent over Mary's religious policies and her marriage to Philip of Spain, an active Catholic.

Elizabeth was suspected of supporting various uprisings throughout Mary's reign. In 1554, following a rebellion led by Sir Thomas Wyatt, son of the poet of the same name associated with Anne Boleyn, she was interrogated and imprisoned in the Tower when it became known that she was 'approached' by some of the rebels. Mary was pressured by the Emperor Charles V's ambassador to put Elizabeth on trial for insurrection as her throne would never be safe. Thankfully, Mary was convinced to spare her, instead putting her under house arrest for a year.

Elizabeth was recalled to court in April 1555 to attend Mary's pregnancy, which could result in Elizabeth's chances of being queen considerably lessened. However, it was a false pregnancy and Elizabeth returned to Hatfield Palace in peace. In 1557 Mary again thought she was pregnant, but there was no child, and during the following year she became very ill.

Elizabeth had been recognised by Mary as her heir, and was starting to make plans for her government. Following Mary's death in November 1558, Elizabeth was declared Queen at the age of 25 and was crowned in Westminster Abbey on 15 January 1559.

Elizabeth, granddaughter of Sir Thomas Boleyn, Earl of Wiltshire, had achieved the pinnacle of the Boleyn ambition.

Elizabeth went on to reign for more than 40 years, although she didn't go unchallenged. One of her first moves was to establish a religious settlement through the Act of Supremacy to re-establish the Church of England, whilst maintaining a degree of tolerance for Catholics. However that wasn't enough to stop attacks from the French and

Elizabeth I, The Armada Portrait, c.1588
Artist unknown. Queens House, Greenwich.

Spanish, who backed a claim on the Crown from Mary, Queen of Scots, who was a great-granddaughter of Henry VII.

Queen Elizabeth survived these many attacks and established a network of international trading links with Russia, North Africa, India, China and the Americas. She never married, despite having many suitors, and bore no children, so there was no immediate heir to the throne.

Elizabeth died on the 25th March 1603 (the last day of the year of 1602 in the old calendar), still with no named heir. Robert Cecil, her chief minister, had been quietly negotiating with James VI of Scotland, son of Mary, Queen of Scots and descendant of Henry VII, and within a few hours of her death, the Privy Council proclaimed James as King of England.

The Tudor era and the Boleyn line had finally come to an end with the crowning of James I.

Blickling Hall, 2024
Image © S. Haines

Chapter 13
A Brief History of Blickling

Blickling Hall, as you see it today, was largely completed in the 17th century by the Hobart family but it is likely that much of the building was constructed by the Boleyns., who owned the estate from 1452 to 1553. Before that there were earlier manor houses on the site.

The name of the estate occurs in the Domesday Book as 'Blikelinges', meaning settlement of the followers of Blicla. In Old English it's called 'Bekeling', a water meadow around a stream.

It was first owned by Harold Godwinson, Earl of the East Saxons and later King of England. He transferred it to his brother Gurth in 1057.

Upon the death of both Harold, King of England, and his brother at the Battle of Hastings in 1066, the estate was seized by William the Conqueror who gave the whole manor to his chaplain Herfast, Bishop of Thetford. It then passed to his successor, Bishop Everard de Calna, who held Blickling as a single manor.

The bishops built a large stone and wood manor house and chapel, with enclosing bank and fishponds, on their portion of the estate to the west of Moorgate, near to the river Bure. It was identified on Corbridge's map of Blickling of 1729 as the 'Old Mannor'. The manor eventually fell out of use and was let to various tenants. Buildings stood here until the 16th century.[1]

In 1144 Bishop Everard sold (or granted) the southern part of the estate to John Fitzherbert, Lord of Norbury.[2]

In 1309 it was purchased by Robert de Holveston. His son James, a collector of taxes in Norfolk (1345-50), moved with his wife Joan into Blickling Manor in 1369, succeeding to his father's full estate in 1378. Having no sons, he left it to Sir Nicholas Dagworth. This is the part of the estate on which the present Blickling Hall is situated.

Sir Nicholas Dagworth was a soldier and diplomat of Edward III and Richard II. He was Richard's ambassador to Pope Urban VI. He settled

---

[1] Parsons, W. L E. (1934). Notes on the Boleyn family. Norfolk Archaeology Vol. 25(3), pp. 386-407.

[2] Landon L., Suffolk Institute, 'Everard, Bishop of Norwich' pp. 186-196

at Blickling in 1390, building a wooden rectangular moated manor house before his death in 1401.

In 1407, Dagworth's widow, Alianora, released all her rights to the manor to Sir Thomas de Erpingham and Sir Robert Berney. At her death, the manor was then in the hands of Erpingham and his feoffees[1]. Erpingham died in 1428 and his executors sold the estate to Sir John Fastolf of Caister Castle in 1432 for £1,647. Blickling was considered a very fine estate, thus the high price. Only Sir Nicholas Dagworth and his family lived at Blickling; for Erpingham and Fastolf, the estate was purely as an investment.

Sir John Fastolf sold the Blickling estate in 1452 for £1,365, plus an annuity of £60 a year, to Sir Geoffrey Boleyn, future lord mayor of the city of London (1457), who made it his country seat. The Boleyns were now at Blickling. Sir Geoffrey also bought Hever Castle and its estate from Fastolf in 1462. Sir Geoffrey's grandson, Thomas, who inherited the estate from his father, William, in 1505, continued to pay a fee of 3s 6d every 30 weeks to the Bishop of Norwich for possession of the northern part of the Blickling estate, which was still owned by the bishops.

There were suggestions at the time that Sir Geoffrey bought Blickling on behalf of John Heydon, a Duke of Suffolk ally in the region, but instead settled here himself with his wife Anne, daughter of Lord Hoo. Once in possession, Sir Geoffrey, along with his son William and grandson Thomas, built a new brick house on the site of Dagworth's wooden mansion. The Boleyns' brick Tudor house was later incorporated into the Jacobean house built by Sir Henry Hobart.[2]

Following Sir William's death in 1505, Thomas and his family moved to Hever, leaving his brother James in occupation at Blickling, although in 1525 the Blickling estate was assigned to Jane Parker (Lady Rochford) as part of the marriage settlement to Thomas's son George.

Thomas died in 1539 leaving the family estates to his brother James and in 1541, on Jane's death, the Blickling estate also reverted to James.

In the 1540s and 50s James consolidated his holdings in Norfolk, exchanging with Henry VIII the Boleyn lands in Kent for grants of monastic land in the Blickling area (in particular the Bishops of Norwich manor at Blickling) bringing the two halves of the original manor back together. James was the last Boleyn to live at Blickling. He died in 1561 and is buried in the family vault in Blickling church.

However, in 1553 James had sold part of the Blickling estate, including the house, to his nephew John Clere, the son of his sister Alice, although he may have continued to live there. But in his will, James stated that Edward Clere, John's son, still owed him £400, so the sale

---

[1] A feoffee was a type of trustee or nominee used to hold property on behalf of another in order to avoid death taxes.

[2] Williamson T. and Dallas P. *The Landscape of the Blickling Estate*, p.15

may have been a way of avoiding death taxes. As James had no direct heir, he left the remainder of his estates to Queen Elizabeth I, his great-niece, who in turn granted her portion of Blickling to Sir Henry Hobart of Intwood in the early 1600s.

The Clere's were to spend much time and money on the building of their palaces at Blickling and Thetford through the 1570s. They eventually went bankrupt in the attempt, having spent most of their monies on their manor house at Thetford where they entertained Queen Elizabeth I and her court in 1578.

In 1615 Sir Henry Hobart bought the estate and transformed the Tudor house into the Jacobean hall that stands at Blickling today.

Life Size Wood Carving of Anne Boleyn
In the stairwell at Blickling Hall. The inscription reads "Anne Boleyn Hic Nata" (Anne Boleyn Born Here").
Image © S. Haines.

Pillars on either side of the main entrance at Blickling Hall with the bull and falcon crests of the Boleyn family.
Images © S. Haines

Holbein Portrait of Henry VIII at Blickling
Image © S. Haines

Acknowledgements

This book is the result of five years of research and loads of reading and searching! It came about because I saw a definite lack of information about the Boleyn family's presence at Blickling when I started volunteering here. They were here for approximately 100 years and yet, were rarely, if ever, mentioned in connection with the estate.

Considering the long term impact and importance this family had on English history, and that a queen of England was born at Blickling I decided to write this book for the benefit of all Blickling's people: staff, volunteers and our visitors. Although many books have been written about Anne, and to a lesser extent her father and siblings, no single book had told the entire story.

This book would not have seen the light of day without the backing of Joy Beresford Frye, author and playwright. Her expertise, skill and patience were instrumental and of great value. And to Steve Haines of Bittern Books, our publisher, for his steadfast support, hard graft and huge patience in getting this book printed. I take my hat off to both.

My thanks as well to the National Archives and the Norfolk Records Office for their research assistance during the five years in preparation of this book. I'm also grateful to Megan Dennis and Jill Morgan for reading the proof copies and giving valuable feedback, and to Sandy Horsley for her wonderful cover design.

Having said that, any errors or omissions are entirely my responsibility.

Chuck Weigand 2025

The image of Anne Boleyn on page 34 is a Hans Holbein the Younger drawing of her while she was still alive held by the Royal Collection. It has been verified by both Eric Ives, her biographer, and the Royal Collection. A copy is displayed at Blickling Hall.

About the Author

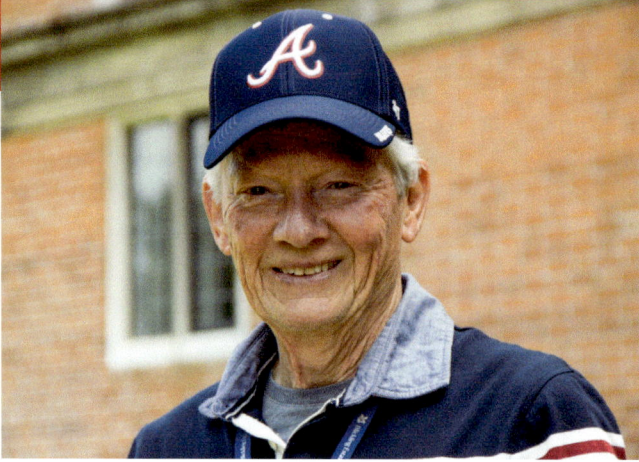

Charles J Weigand (Chuck) was born on the 11th June 1945 in Brooklyn, New York. His father was a Lieutenant in the Navy who died in a plane crash at Kwajalein Lagoon in the Pacific in February 1945 on his way to an aircraft carrier assignment.

At 17, Chuck joined the US Navy, looking to follow in his father's footsteps. In his 21 year Navy career, he became a telecommunications specialist, served on five Navy ships and traveled around the world, from Norfolk, Virginia, to Guam in the Mariana Islands.

Upon retiring from the Navy in 1983, Chuck was employed by the US National Security Agency (NSA) in their telecommunications center. During 19 years with the NSA he worked in computer security, counter espionage, code breaking, and US embassy communications center inspections.

Chuck retired again in 2002, this time in England, eventually ending up in Norfolk where he started working as a Blickling Hall Room Guide and researcher:

"I have been volunteering at Blickling for eight years and love it. History, specifically Tudor, has been my passion and hobby for most of my life."

If you visit Blickling, you will often find Chuck in his present role as Ambassador greeting visitors at the entrance to the house.

Bibliography

Primary Sources

Calendar of State Papers, Spain (CSPS in footnotes)
– British History Online at https://www.british-history.ac.uk/series/calendar-state-papers-spain

Letters and Papers, Foreign and Domestic, Henry VIII (LP in footnotes)
– British History Online at https://www.british-history.ac.uk/series/letters-and-papers-henry-viii

Secondary Sources

Bell, Doyne c.:
– Notices of the Historic Persons Buried in the Chapel of St. Peter Ad Vincula in the Tower of London

Borman, Tracy:
– The Private Lives of the Tudors (Hodder 2017)
– Thomas Cromwell (Hodder 2015)
– Anne Boleyn and Elizabeth I (Hodder 2024)

Chapman, Andrew (ed):
– Thomas Cromwell: A Historical Sourcebook (Hertitage Hunter 2020)

Cherry, Claire and Ridgway, Claire:
– - George Boleyn: Tudor Poet, Courtier And Diplomat (MadeGlobal 2014)

Clark, Dr. Michael MP:
– Rochford Hall, The History of a Tudor House (Stroud Sutton 1990)

Cunningham, S.,
– How to kill a queen?, 2020, https://blog.nationalarchives.gov.uk/how-to-kill-a-queen-preparing-for-the-execution-of-anne-boleyn-in-may-1536/

Emerson, Dr. Owen and Ridgway, Claire:
– The Boleyns of Hever Castle. (MadeGlobal 2021)

Fox, Julia:
– Jane Boleyn: The Infamous Lady Rochford (Orion 2009)

Griffiths, Elizabeth:
– The Boleyns at Blickling, 1450-1560 (Norfolk Archaeology XLV 2009, 453-68)

Heale, Elizabeth:
– The Devonshire Manuscript: A women's book of courtly poetry (Toronto, 2012)

Ives, Eric:
– The Life and Death of Anne Boleyn (Wiley-Blackwell 2005)

Grueninger, Natalie:
– The Final Year of Anne Boleyn (Pen & Sword 2022)

Licence, Amy:
– 1520: The Field of the Cloth of Gold (Amberley 2020)

Loades, Professor David:
– The Boleyns: The Rise and Fall of a Tudor Family (Amberley 2012)

MacCulloch, Diarmid:
– Thomas Cranmer: A Life (Yale 1997)

Mackay, Lauren:
– Among the Wolves of Court (Bloomsbury 2018)
– Inside the Tudor Court (Amberley 2015)

Martin, Claire:
– Heirs of Ambition: The Making of the Boleyns (History Press, 2023)

Moyle, Franny:
– The King's Painter: The Life and Times of Hans Holbein (Apollo 2022)

Norton, Elizabeth:
– The Boleyn Women (Amberley 2013)
– The Lives of Tudor Women (Head of Zeus 2017)
– Anne Boleyn: In Her Own Words and the Words of Those Who Knew Her (Amberley 2011)

O'Day, Rosemary:
– The Routledge Companion to The Tudor Age (Routledge 2010)

Soberton, Sylvia Barbara:
– Ladies in Waiting: Women Who Served Anne Boleyn (Golden Age 2022)

Starkey, David:
– Six Wives: The Queens of Henry VIII (Vintage 2004)
– The Reign of Henry VIII: Personalities and Politics (Hamlyn 1985)

Taffe, James
– Courting Scandal: The Rise and Fall of Jane Boleyn, Lady Rochford (Independently published, 2023)

Thurley, Professor Simon, CBE:
– Tudor Ambition: Houses of the Boleyn Family (Gresham Lecture, 2020. https://www.gresham.ac.uk/watch-now/boleyn-houses)

Weir, Alison:
– The Lady in the Tower: The Fall of Anne Boleyn (Vintage 2010)
– Mary Boleyn: The Great and Infamous Whore (Vintage 2012)

Index